HANDBOOK OF
VASTU

B. NIRANJAN BABU

UBSPD

UBS Publishers' Distributors Ltd.

New Delhi • Mumbai • Bangalore • Chennai •
Calcutta • Patna • Kanpur • London

UBS Publishers' Distributors Ltd.

5 Ansari Road, New Delhi-110 002
Phones : 3273601, 3266646 ☆ *Cable* : ALLBOOKS ☆ *Fax* : (91) 11-327-6593
e-mail: ubspd.del@smy.sprintrpg.ems.vsnl.net.in
Internet: www.ubspd.com
Apeejay Chambers, 5 Wallace Street, Mumbai-400 001
Phones : 2076971, 2077700 ☆ *Cable* : UBSIPUB ☆ *Fax* : 2070827
10 First Main Road, Gandhi Nagar, Bangalore-560 009
Phones : 2263901, 2263902, 2253903 ☆ *Cable* : ALLBOOKS ☆ *Fax* : 2263904
6, Sivaganga Road, Nungambakkam, Chennai-600 034
Phone : 8276355, 8270189 ☆ *Cable* : UBSIPUB ☆ *Fax* : 8278920
8/1-B, Chowringhee Lane, Calcutta-700 016
Phones : 2441821, 2442910, 2449473 ☆ *Cable* : UBSIPUBS ☆ *Fax* : 2450027
5 A, Rajendra Nagar, Patna-800 016
Phones : 672856, 673973, 656170 ☆ *Cable* : UBSPUB ☆ *Fax* : 656169
80, Noronha Road, Cantonment, Kanpur-208 004
Phones : 369124, 362665, 357488 ☆ *Fax* : ᴐ15122

Copyright © B. Niranjan Babu

First Published	1997
First Reprint	1997
Second Reprint	1998
Third Reprint	1998

B. Niranjan Babu asserts the moral right to be identified as
the author of this work.

Printed at Pauls Press, Okhla Industrial Estate, New Delhi, (India).

This book is respectfully
dedicated to my revered parents
Dr. B. V. Raman and Smt. Rajeswari Raman

CONTENTS

CONTENTS

PREFACE

It gives me great pleasure to present herewith my maiden book **Handbook of Vastu.**

In the last few years, Vastu Shastra has become popular and many books have been published on it. Many seminars and symposia have been conducted on it. Buildings also have been modified on Vastu principles with good results.

The awareness of the importance of Vastu Shastra can be said to be recent though the science itself is ancient.

I have endeavoured to put before the readers the basic principles of Vastu as expounded by classical authorities. Relevant diagrams and tables have been provided to enable the reader to understand the principles better.

The book is divided into five sections: The first three sections are further divided into chapters and each chapter begins with an 'at a glance' paragraph. The fourth section answers some common queries related to construction and modification of houses. A few illustrative building plans in the fifth section will, no doubt, enable the reader to grasp the principles better.

I hope the reader will be enabled to acquire a working knowledge of Vastu by studying this book.

My study and research in Vastu have been solely due to the encouragement and guidance of my revered parents Dr. B. V. Raman and Mrs. Rajeswari Raman.

I express my thanks to several friends whose suggestions have helped me in the writing of this book.

— **B. NIRANJAN BABU**

FOREWORD

It is with pleasure that I am writing the following words by way of a Foreword to my son B. Niranjan Babu's work "Handbook of Vastu".

In Sanskrit Vastu ordinarily means a dwelling house. It also denotes the plot of land over which a dwelling house is built. Silpa Sastras and astrological works deal with this subject exhaustively.

Niranjan Babu has made a careful study of most of the extant classical literature and appears to have a firm grip on the subject.

It is necessary that houses, factories, hotels etc., are constructed according to Vastu so that destructive vibrations emanating from Nature due to the materials used are screened off.

The book takes the reader in a graduated form through the essentials of Vastu and its practical application. Several diagrams are given to enable one to put to practical use, the principles of Vastu.

The author has already made his mark in the field of Vastu and bids to hold his own in the future. I am glad to say that this work has been done with considerable skill and ability.

Today, the market is being flooded with several books on the subject; but the present one fulfills a long-felt want for its clarity and style of presentation, I bid my son God-speed in his efforts to propagate and promote Vastu for the good of all those who are interested in it.

Bangalore
16-3-1997
                                                    B. V. RAMAN

SECTION I

1. Introduction

> ### *At a glance:*
>
> *Vastu is the science of architecture. It dates back to pre-ramayana and Mahabharatha periods. Eighteen professors of Vastu are mentioned in the* **Matsya Purana** *. Some of the important works on Vastu are* **Manasara, Mayamata, Brihat Samhita, Viswakarma Prakasha and Samarangana Sutradhara**.

Vastu (pronounced as Vaastu) is defined as a dwelling in the Sanskrit dictionary. Amarakosha of Amarasimha defines Shastra as a treatise. Vastu Shastra therefore means the treatise on dwellings or the science of architecture.

As **Manasara** (a great work on Ancient Architecture) puts it, architecture broadly means the ground (*dhara*), the building or edifice (*harmya*), the conveyance (*yana*) and the bedstead (*paryaka*) and other couches.

The principles of Vastu as enumerated in classical texts are universally applicable irrespective of religion or place. These principles can be adapted to suit modern conditions. Vastu's concern is not only material prosperity but also mental peace and happiness and harmony in the family, office etc.

Vastu is also an integral point of Jyotisha. **Mayamata** says: "The house is to be entered at an auspicious time which accords with the owner's horoscope after doing the propitiatory rites." According to Dr. Raman, editor of THE ASTROLOGICAL MAGAZINE, the fourth house in an astrological chart has reference to mother, *immovable property*, education, *vehicles* and general happiness. Dr. Raman says: "It follows as a matter of course that an affliction to the fourth house may result in the shape of depriving the person of peace of mind, troubles in regard to property affairs and so on. He may command good immoveable property but may not be happy".

The science of Vastu takes into primordial consideration the energies radiating from the four directions, viz., North, East, South and West. It explains in simple language the selection of site, the construction of a dwelling and the placement of the various rooms in the dwelling for bettering our lives.

Morris Schindler, a Philadelphia architect who has built houses based on Vastu principles (Sthapatya Veda) says: "In particular, the design of a space should actually stimulate one to feel the quintessential qualities of its intended purposes . . . . For example, the dining room should stimulate the experience of hunger, the living room sociability, the study alertness and the bedroom rest."

This book is intended to give the reader the basic principles of Vastu, and how it can be applied to better our lives.

If one follows the broad principles given in the pages of this book while constructing one's house or industry or while doing the interiors of one's office, shop, clinic, hotel, etc one can look forward to better times.

Our ancients had great forethought. They knew that one of the basic needs of man, viz., shelter if taken care of carefully in accordance with the principles of Vastu, man would be stronger to face life's complexities.

Many of the great temples and palaces of India are remark-able legacies of ancient India and bear testimony to the great-ness of this ancient science of architecture.

Vastu dates back to the Pre-Ramayana and the Mahabharata periods. The Epics contain description of cities with multistoreyed buildings with spacious balconies and porticoes. It is said that the site plan of Ayodhya city was similar to the plan found in the great architectural text **Manasara**.

In the Mahabharata it is said a number of houses were built for the kings who were invited to Indraprastha for the Rajasuya Yagna of King Yuddhistira. Sage Vyasa says that these houses were as high as the peaks of Kailasa Mountains, perhaps meaning that they stood tall and majestic. The houses were free from obstructions, had compounds with high walls and their doors were of uniform height and inlaid with numerous metal ornaments.

References are also to be found in Buddhist literature, of buildings constructed on the basis of Vastu. The Jatakas contain detached references to individual buildings. Lord Buddha, is said to have delivered discourses on architecture and even told his disciples that supervising the construction of a building was one of the duties of the order.

Mention is made of Viharas or monasteries or temples, *Ardhayogas* or buildings which are partly residential and partly religious, *Prasadas* or residential storeyed buildings, harmyas which are also multi-storeyed buildings and *Guhas* or residential buildings for middle class people.

A treatise known as *Chullavagga* with a commentary of Buddhaghosa is said to contain much material on the science of architecture.

Many Puranas such as Skanda, Agni, Matsya, Garuda, Narada, Vayu, Brahmanda and Linga, deal with Vastu fairly extensively.

For instance the **Matsyapurana** refers to eighteen sages proficient in Vastu.

Bhriguratri Vasishtascha Viswakarma Mayaasthatha |
Narado Nagnajichaiva Visalaakshaha Purandaraha ||

Brahma Kumaro Nandeesha Shaunako Gaarga Eva Cha |
Vaasudevo Anirudhascha thatha Sukro Brihaspatihi ||
Ashtaadashaite Vijyaatha Vastushastropadeshakaha ||

भृगुरात्रि वसिष्ठाश्च विश्वकर्म मयास्तथा ।
नारदो नग्नाजिच्चैव विसालाक्षः पुरन्दरः ॥
ब्रह्मा कुमारो नन्दीशा शौनको गार्ग एव च ।
वासुदेवो अनिरुद्धाश्च तथा शुक्रो बृहस्पतिः ॥
अष्टादशैते विज्ञाते वास्तुशास्त्रोपदेशकः ॥

(Bhrigu, Atri, Vasishta, Viwakarma, Maya, Narada, Nagnajitha, Visalaaksha, Purandhara, Brahma, Kumara, Nandisa, Saunaka, Gaarga, Vaasudeva, Aniruddha, Sukra and Brihaspati are the eighteen celebrated authors referred to as Vastu Shastropadesakas or instructors in the Science of Vastu.)

In the **Brihat Samhita**, Chapters 53 and 56 exquisitely deal with residential and temple architecture.

In this classic, reference is made to underground water and how to divine it. Various methods detail the exploration of water springs. Stanza 40 says that:

वल्मीकसंवृतो यदि तालो वा भवति नालिकेरो वा ।
पश्चात् षड्भिर्हस्तैर्नरैश्चतुर्भिः शिरा याम्या ॥

If a palm or coconut tree is found to be covered with anthills, a southerly water-vein is present at a depth of 20 cubits and at a distance of 6 cubits from the tree.

Another important factor to note is that this classic recommends water tanks or sumps to have their eastern and western sides longer than the southern and northern sides.

It is also interesting to note the preparation and use of an adamantine glue (akin to the modern day cement) to be used in construction of residential buildings, temples and idols finds a prominent place.

The various Agamas also give much useful information on architecture. Notable among them are *Kamikagama, Karnagama, Suprabhedagama, Vaikhansagama* and *Amsumadbhedagama*.

Certain works on Tantra such as *Kirana Tantra* and *Hayaseersha Tantra* are also said to contain much information on architecture.

Other treatises like Kautilya's *Arthasastra* and *Sukra Niti* are said to dwell on structural aspects of architecture.

Some of the more important works on the science of dwelling are **Manasara** and **Samarangana Sutradhara, Mayamata**.

Manasara is a comprehensive treatise on architecture and iconography. According to Mr. P. K. Acharya, the editor of **Manasara**, this book is considered to be the source of all presentations of architecture in Purana and Agama as well as in more specialised texts such as **Brihat Samhita** and **Mayamata**. In fact this treatise itself is identified as a Vastu Sastra, the first Vastu being the earth.

Manasara represents the universality of Vastu tradition and contains also the iconography of Jain and Buddhist images. The work is universally accepted all over India.

Manasara, a great exposition on the science of Vastu or architecture uses the term **Manasara** in three distinct ways, namely, the author of an unknown time and parentage, a class of sages or rishis who deal with the essence of measurement or mana-sara and lastly a treatise containing methods and rules of architectural and sculptural construction. Prof. P.K. Acharya has exhaustively and painstakingly translated this classic work into English. The professor attempts to date the **Manasara** to a few centuries earlier to the Christian era.

Manasara makes use of two main units of measurement. The *angula* or the breadth of a thumb (roughly 3/4 of an inch and *hasta* (24 angulas) for architectural measure and *taala* (the span between the tips of a fully stretched thumb and middle finger) for sculptural measure.

Four types of architects are defined. The chief architect (Sthapathi), the designer or draftsman (Sutragrahin), the Painter (Vardhanthi) and the Carpenter (Sutradhara). Just as Varahamihira in his **Brihat Jataka** prescribes the qualifications of an astrologer, **Manasara** too prescribes certain qualifications for an architect. An architect should have novel ideas, be apt in acquisition of knowledge, be a good writer, a skillful draftsman, versed in geometry and optics, informed in the principles of natural and moral philosophy, not ignorant of the sciences of law and physics and most important he should also be well versed in astronomy - astrology and mathematics.

Manasara also evaluates merits and demerits with the following sloka.

Yatra Dosho Gunadhikyam Tatra Dosho Na Vidhyate
Teshamadhikagunaam Vaanamyam Sarvadoshakaram Bhavet

meaning when the merit is more than demerit, there is no defect in it; but if the demerit is more than the merit, it would be all defective.

Samarangana Sutradhara is authored by King Bhoja (of Dhara) who ruled between 1018 AD to 1060 AD. He was a great patron of poets and men of letters. In addition to **Samarangana Sutradhara**, he is said to have written 33 other works on a variety of subjects like astronomy, poetics, philosophy, politics, Dharma Sastra, Drama, Architecture, Grammar, Medicine, Saivisim, etc.

Samarangana Sutradhara is a remarkable legacy of King Bhoja. His rule was noted for splendour and grandeur. This great work not only deals with house architecture, town planning and temple architecture but also deals with the canons of painting and mechanical devices known as Yantras. It consists of 83 chapters.

Mayamata of Maya also deals extensively and exhaustively with the subject of architecture with reference to dwelling sites, examination of the soil, systems of measurement and orientation, villages and towns, the building of temples, etc. It discusses the importance of doors, gateways and pavilions besides vehicles, beds and seats.

Mayamata has quite a few references to the position of a well. Invariably these slokas recommend the placement of wells either in the north, north east or east of the plot.

Mayamata occupies a very important place amongst the various treatises on Vastu. It is said to have originated from South India. It is the best known among the ancient treatises dealing with architecture and iconography. Maya, the author was not only an expert in Vastu but also in Jyothisha. The famous astronomical **Surya Siddhanta** is also authored by Maya.

Vishwa Karma Vastu shastra is a treatise to which reference is made to by Varahamihira as early as the sixth century AD. This treatise deals systematically with orientation of sites, men and materials to be employed in vastu, examination of soil, town and village planning, temple construction or prasadas, construction of palaces, bhavanas or mansions, the anthapura or inner chambers in a royal palace.

One of the chapters also deals with the dining hall, the placement of seats and the directions there of.

There are ever so many other rare, seen and unseen works on this great science like the *Silparatna, Aparajitha Praccha* etc.

The classical works referred to speak of **Aya**. Every plot and building is said to have life and hence has to be built to perfect proportions based on certain formulae. When a building is so constructed, it is ensured of long life and the residents live happily with good health, wealth and prosperity. These formulae called the Ayadi Shadvarga are 1) Aya, Increase or profit 2) Vyaya, decrease or loss 3) Rksa or Nakshatra 4) Yoni or source or the orientation of the building 5) Vara (week day) or the solar day and 6) Tithi or the lunar day.

Our ancients were not hair splitting philosophers but men of intuitive and scholarly abilities. They had made great strides in the science of not only architecture but also in Jyotisha, Vedanta, Yoga, etc.

Even today we have great monumental temples in India like the Vidyasankara temple of Sringeri, the Rameswaram temple, the Meenakshi temple of Madurai, the Venkateswara temple of Tirumala, the Brihadeeswara Temple of Tanjore and many others which have withstood the onslaught of time. These temples are visited by thousands of people with all sorts of problems day in and day out who return back to their homes with mental solace and peace.

Vastu Shastra is a great science of architecture that was founded by our ancients for a comfortable and contented society at large. Pyramids, mirrors and yantras are not on integral part of Vastu but may only *aid* in Vastu's goal of achieving a healthy, wealthy and prosperous world.

2. Who is the Vastu Purusha

At a glance:

Vastu Purusha is the diety ruling the plot. The three types of Vastu are Nitya Vastu, Chara Vastu, Sthira Vastu. Sthira Vastu is considered in the permanent aspects of building.

Brihat Samhita, Chapter LIII, Slokas 2,3 says:

किमपि किल भूतमभवदुन्धानं रोदसी शरीरेण ।
तदमरगणेन सहसा विनिगृह्याधोमुखं न्यस्तम् ॥
यत्र च येन गृहीतं विबुधेनाधिष्ठितः स तत्रैव ।
तदमरमयं विधाता वास्तुनरं कल्पयामास ॥

It is said some Being obstructed the earth and the sky with its body. The gods suddenly caught the being and laid it face down. Whichever limbs were held by different gods had those very gods as their presiding dieties. The creator ordered that the Being be the god of the plot (or house).

The story also runs as follows: When Lord Shiva is fighting the demon called Andhaka, his (the Lord's) perspiration falls to the ground. Out of this is born the Vastu Purusha. Being hungry he starts devouring everything that comes his way. The gods then go to Lord Brahma. He tells them to hold the 'being' face down. 45 deities press him down. Lord Brahma blesses him saying that he will be the deity of all plots and offerings have to be done to him. In return Vastu Purusha is said to take care of the inmates of the house.

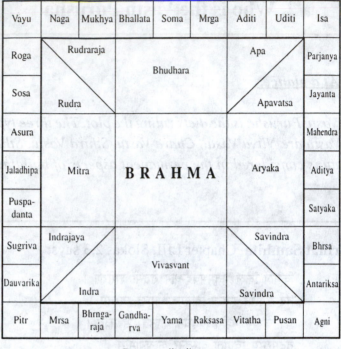

Vayu	Naga	Mukhya	Bhallata	Soma	Mrga	Aditi	Uditi	Isa
Roga	Rudraraja			Bhudhara		Apa		Parjanya
Sosa		Rudra					Apavatsa	Jayanta
Asura								Mahendra
Jaladhipa		Mitra		**BRAHMA**		Aryaka		Aditya
Puspa-danta								Satyaka
Sugriva	Indrajaya			Vivasvant		Savindra		Bhrsa
Dauvarika		Indra					Savindra	Antariksa
Pitr	Mrsa	Bhrnga-raja	Gandha-rva	Yama	Raksasa	Vitatha	Pusan	Agni

Paramasayika diagram

Fig 2.01

The above figure names the dieties responsible to keep the Vastu Purusha on the plot.

The Vastu Purusha is said to have three positions viz., 1) Nitya Vastu 2) Chara Vastu and 3) Sthira Vastu.

Nitya Vastu

The Vastu Purusha's gaze changes every three hours in a day.

Chara Vastu

The Vastu Purusha's gaze is directed towards South during *Bhadrapada, Ashwayuja* and *Karthika* corresponding to September, October, November and December months; towards West during *Margasira, Pushya* and *Magha* corresponding to

December, January, February and March months; towards North during *Phalguna, Chaitra* and *Vaishaka* corresponding to March, April, May and June months and towards East during *Jyeshta, Ashada* and *Shravana* corresponding to June, July, August and September months.

Research students will observe that Vastu Purusha's change of position are closely linked to the various seasonal changes.

Sthira Vastu

The third and most important position is the Sthira Vastu where his position is as below.

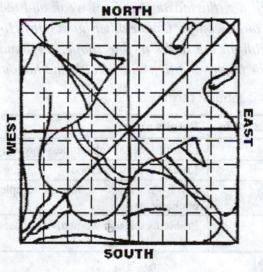

Fig No.2.02

Here his feet are on the South-west, his left arm on the North-west, his head on the North-east and his right arm on the South-east.

As the name implies Sthira Vastu is concerned with the construction of a house, temple, village, town, etc and their permanence.

Brihat Samhita clearly recommends a square or rectangle site with the following sloka.

दक्षिणाभुजेन हीने वास्तुनरेऽर्थक्षयोऽङ्गनादोषाः ।
वामेऽर्थधान्यहानिः शिरसि गुणैर्हीयते सर्वैः ॥
स्त्रीदोषाः सुतमरणं प्रेष्यत्वं चापि चरणावैकल्ये ।
अविकलपुरुषे वसतां मानार्थयुतानि सौख्यानि ॥

If the "Vastu Nara" god has no right arm, the owner will lose wealth and will be miserable through women. If he is without the left arm, there is loss of money and food. If his head is absent, he will fall from all virtues. If his feet are missing male children will die, the master becomes weak and there will be troubles through women. On the other hand if the House god is endowed with all the limbs in fine shape, the inmates of the house will be happy and live with wealth and honour.

Putting this is tabular form

If the plot is cut in	Results are
South-east	Loss of wealth, unhappiness through women
North-west	Loss of money and food
North-east	Fall from virtues - no morals, scruples or character
South-west	Problems through women, likely death of sons and servile attitude.

Table 2.01

3. Understanding Directions

At a glance:

Selection of a site involves the understanding of the eight directions.

Before we go in for selection of a site let us understand the various directions with the help of the following diagram. This diagram is referred to as *Pitha* in **Mayamata**.

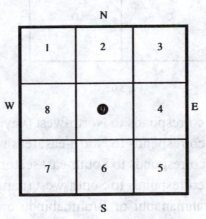

Fig 3.01

1   refers to North-west (vayuvya)
2   refers to North (uttara)
3   refers to North-east (eashanya)
4   refers to East (Poorva)
5   refers to South-east (Agneya)

6   refers to South (dakshina)

7   refers to South-west (nairutya)

8   refers to West (paschima) and

9   refers to Brahmasthana (the central portion) or the
space around the navel of the Vastu Purusha.

Similarly when we talk of the sectors the following diagram
called *Pechaka* is self explanatory.

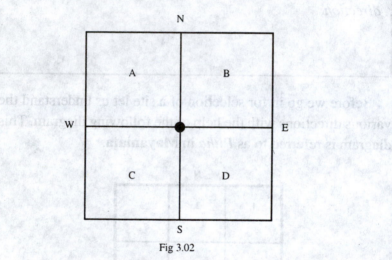

Fig 3.02

1   A corresponds to North-west (vayuvya) sector

2   B corresponds to North-east (eashanya) sector

3   C corresponds to South-east sector (Agneya) and

4   D corresponds to South-west (nairutya) sector

●   Brahmanabhi or Brahmabindu or the centre of
        gravity of the plot.

4. Selection of site

At a glance:

Select a properly oriented site. Avoid irregularly shaped plots. Avoid places of disturbance. Test the soil for suitability construction. Square or rectangles are good.

Selection of a site is very important. Just as you would take care to select a bride or groom, be equally cautious while selecting your site. Avoid buying plots which are not oriented to cardinal directions.

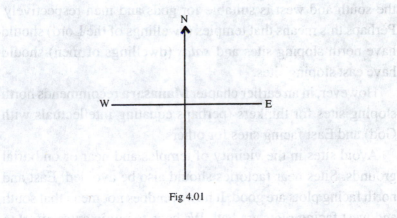

Fig 4.01

Select Rectangular or Square sites.

For rectangular sites let not the length be more than twice the width. **Mayamata**, however prescribes a ratio of 1:1.25.

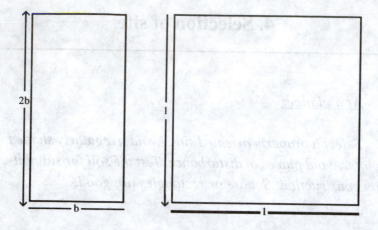

Fig 4.02

Sites which slope towards north and east are said to be good for health, wealth and success in life.

Manasara says that quadrangular ground elevated towards the south and west is suitable for gods and men respectively. Perhaps this means that temples (dwellings of the Lord) should have north sloping sites and *salas* (dwellings of men) should have east sloping sites.

However, in an earlier chapter **Manasara** recommends north sloping sites for thinkers (perhaps equating intellectuals with God) and East facing sites for others.

Avoid sites in the vicinity of temples and near or on burial grounds. Sites near factories should also be avoided. East and north facing plots are good. It however does not mean that south and west facing plots are bad. We have to put in extra effort to give vastu strength to the plot. The plot need not be rejected.

Suppose a site that has the North and/or east elevated has already been purchased. The plot can be rectified by levelling the plot.

Avoid plots in the shape of
1) Triangle

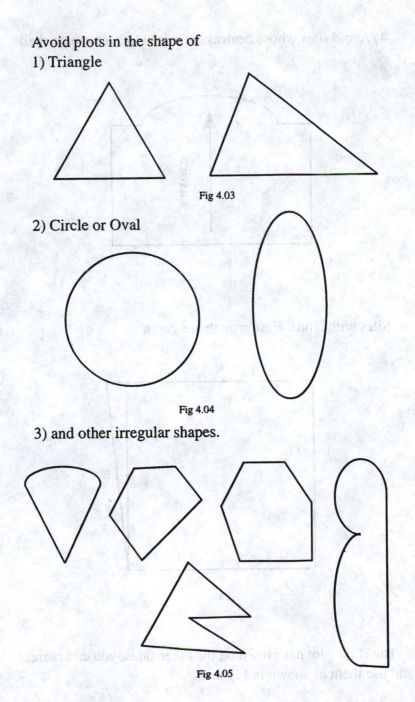

Fig 4.03

2) Circle or Oval

Fig 4.04

3) and other irregular shapes.

Fig 4.05

4) Avoid sites whose centres are raised like a tortoise shell.

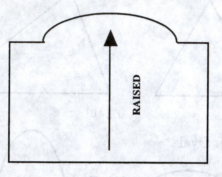

Fig 4.06

Sites with North-East growth are good.

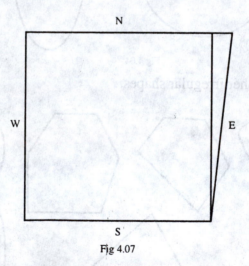

Fig 4.07

But if the plot has grown on the other sides, you can correct and use them as shown in Fig 4.08.

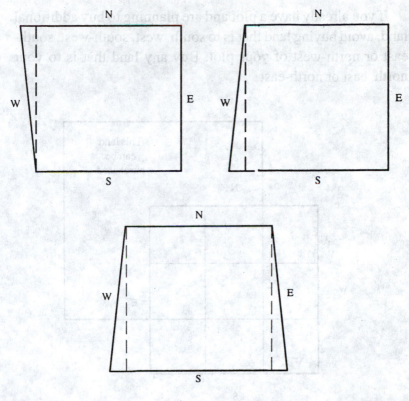

Fig 4.08

Avoid purchasing smaller plots in between two bigger plots.

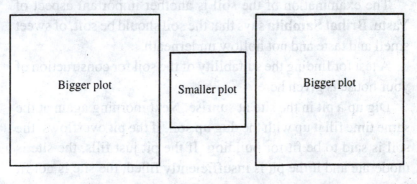

Fig 4.09

If you already have a plot and are planning to buy additional land, avoid buying land that is to south, west, south-west, south-east or north-west of your plot. Buy any land that is to your north, east or north-east.

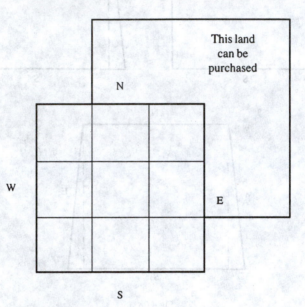

Fig 4.10

The examination of the soil is another important aspect of Vastu. **Brihat Samhita** says that the soil should be soft, of sweet smell and taste and not hollow underneath.

A test for finding the suitability of the soil for construction of your house is given here.

Dig up a pit in the site at sunrise. Next morning again at the same time fill it up with the dug up soil. If the pit overflows, the soil is said to be fit for building. If the pit just fills, the site is moderate and if the pit is insufficiently filled, the site is not fit for construction.

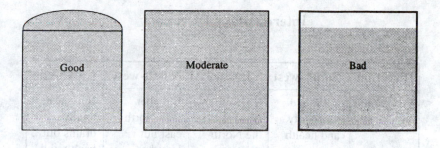

Fig 4.11

The following table gives likely results of elevation and depressions of the site.

Main Directions

Direction	South	North	West	East
Elevation (Slopes up)	Healthy Wealthy Prosperous	Creates miserable monetary situation	Gives good children and fame	Unhappiness from children
Depression (Slopes down)	Severe Ill-health and monetary problems	Generally prosperous and healthy	Education suffers, financial weakness, Bad reputation, Expenditure on medical bills	Keeps you in fit health and makes you prosperous

Table 4.01

Intermediary Directions

Direction	South-west	South-east	North-west	North-east
Elevation	All round prosperity and health	If elevation is more than the North-west and South-east but less than South-west financial strength is obtained	If higher than North-east but less than South-west and South-east general welfare and contentment will be there	If highest, totally drains out health and wealth.
Depression	Master, wife or eldest son becomes weak physically and otherwise.	If lowest fires, frauds and extreme difference of opinions.	If lower than North-east ill health	If lowest, all round prosperity and health

Table 4.02

5. Veedhi shoola

At a glance:

Veedhi Shoolas are roads which thrust into a site. There are favourable and unfavourable Veedhi shoolas.

Shoola is the spear. Veedhi shoola means a road that terminates as dead end to a plot or the house on it. The following table gives the favourable and unfavourable Veedhi shoolas.

Veedhi shoolas	Favourable
North of north-east	Yes
East of north-east	Yes
South of south-east	Yes
East of south-east	No
North of north-west	No
West of north-west	Yes
West of south-west	No
South of south-west	No

Table 5.01

The diagrams Figs 5.01 and 5.02 on the next page help in a better understanding.

Favourable Veedhi Shoolas

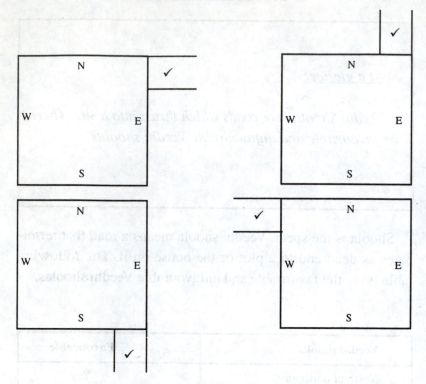

Fig 5.01

Unfavourable Veedhi Shoolas

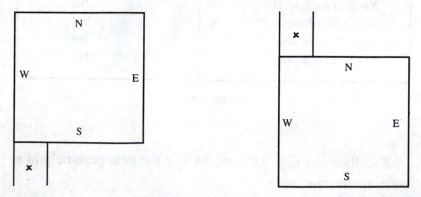

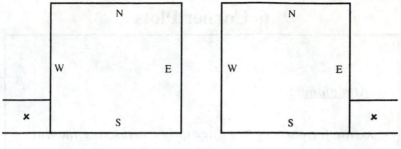

Fig 5.02

While selecting the plot, carefully consider the direction from which the road juts into your plot. As explained above, you can settle for plots which have the following Veedhi Shoola.

1. North of north-east ⟶ Best
2. East of north-east ⟶ Best
3. South of south-east ⟶ Moderate
4. West of north-west ⟶ Moderate

6. Corner Plots

At a glance:

Settle for corner plots after duly considering the directions.

People tend to go in for corner plots so that they have the advantage of open space on two sides. While it is good to go in for corner plots, you need to be careful in selecting the right vastu approved corner plot. North-east corner plots are the best.

As far as possible avoid the other corner plots, viz., south-east, north-west and south-west.

The following results are normally attributed to the corner plots.

Plot	North-east	South-east	North-west	South-west
Result	Generally healthy and prosperous (contented)	Tensions and monetary problems	Addictions, bad thoughts and mercurial in thinking	Master, eldest son weakened

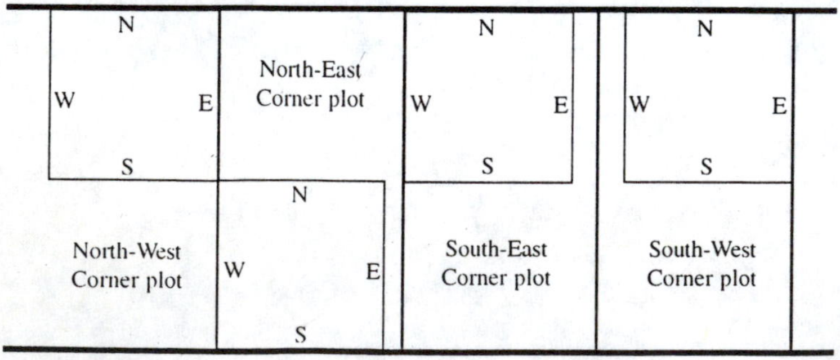

Fig 6.01

However if you are already living in the corner plots not recommended, by proper application of vastu principles to your building, you can minimise/eliminate the drawbacks.

Once the selection of the site is done, the plot has to be thoroughly ploughed and levelled wherever necessary. The ploughing should be done at an auspicious time and due attention should be paid to remove nails, hair, bones and other rubbish, litter etc.

7. Orientation

At a glance:

Always orient building to the cardinal directions. The Shanku is used for finding the orientation. There are three types of Sankhu, viz., Uttama, Madhyama and Adhama.

The compound wall and the building should perfectly orient themselves to the four cardinal directions, viz., east, west, north and south.

The classical texts like **Mayamata**, **Manasara** describe methods of orienting the building (and the compound walls) with the help of a Gnomon. A Gnomon or Sankhu is made of ivory, sandalwood or wood. Three types of Sankhu are mentioned:

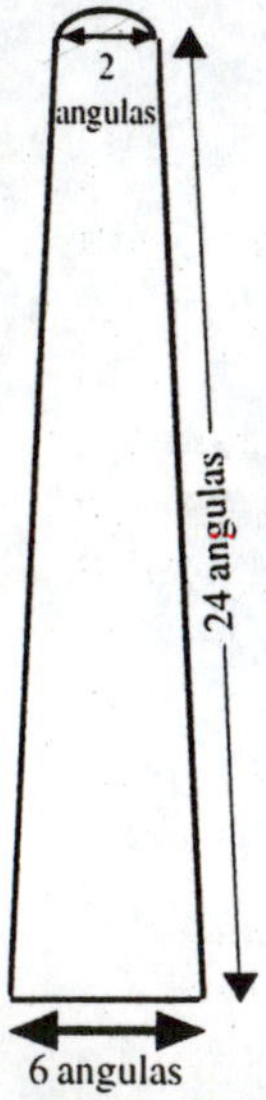

1. **Uttama:** This is 24 angulas (18") high, 6 angulas (4") wide at the base and 2 angulas ($1\frac{1}{2}$") at the top.

2. **Madhyama:** This is 18 angulas ($13\frac{1}{2}$") high, 5 angulas ($3\frac{3}{4}$") wide at the base and one angula ($\frac{3}{4}$") wide at the top.

3. **Adhama:** This is 12 angulas high, four angulas wide at the base and $\frac{1}{3}$ angula wide at the top. The tip should be perfectly shaped.

The middle of the selected site should be cleaned and a square of 2 cubits (36") should be levelled in the centre of which the Sankhu is placed.

2 angulas

24 angulas

6 angulas
UTTAMA
SANKHU

Fig 7.01

At Sunrise, the gnomon or Sankhu is placed at the chosen place. A circle with twice the length of the Sankhu as radius is drawn round the Sankhu.

In the forenoon, the point at which the shadow of the Sankhu touches the circle is marked. Similarly the point at which the shadow touches the circle in the afternoon is marked. The line joining the two points is the east west line.

From each of the east and west points a circle with their distance as radius is drawn. The two intersecting points which are the head and tail of the fish are the north and south points.

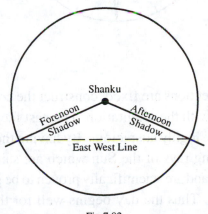

Fig 7.02

Mention is made of the apachchaya and its ommission while marking the length of the shadow. The apachchhaya which can be interpreted as a penumbra (a light or dim shadow) is distinct from the *chhaya* or umbra (dark shadow). The demarcation between the two is very thin and rarely possible to measure.

Therefore the sankhu can be used during the months of August and September corresponding to Kanya or April and May corresponding to Vrishabha.

The modern simpler method is by using the compass which indicate the directions without much effort.

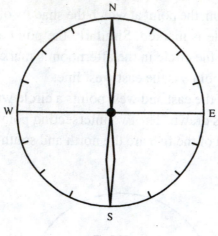

Fig 7.03

Once the directions are fixed, construct the compound walls exactly in line with the orientation. The east facing building is considered to be highly auspicious. By having the building face east, the morning rays of the Sun which are said to consist of ultra violet rays and are scientifically proven to be good for health enter the house. Thus the day begins well for the residents of the house.

8. Offerings to the Plot diety

At a glance:

Clean the plot and make the necessary offerings to the plot diety in the prescribed manner.

The classical works advocate that offerings should be made to the places of the various dieties represented in the diagram (Fig.8.01 in the next page) in beginning from Brahma.

Before the offerings are made the plot is cleaned and the plan made on the ground.

The offerings are brought by a young girl and the architect or the *archaka* (priest) makes the offerings to the dieties by pronouncing their names separately with the mystic syllable *Om* at the beginning and *Namah* at the end. For eg., *Om Brahmaya Namah.*

The offerings normally consist of perfumes, garlands, incense, milk, honey, ghee, milk boiled rice, roasted rice, fruits, curd, durva grass, clarified butter, vegetables, sesame seeds, lotus flowers, etc.

Pandits well versed in the scriptures will be able to guide you on how exactly the offerings are to be made.

The **Manasara** says if the offerings are not made, there will be unhappiness. On the other hand if the dieties are appeased by the offerings, there will always be affluence, peace of mind, harmony and well-being.

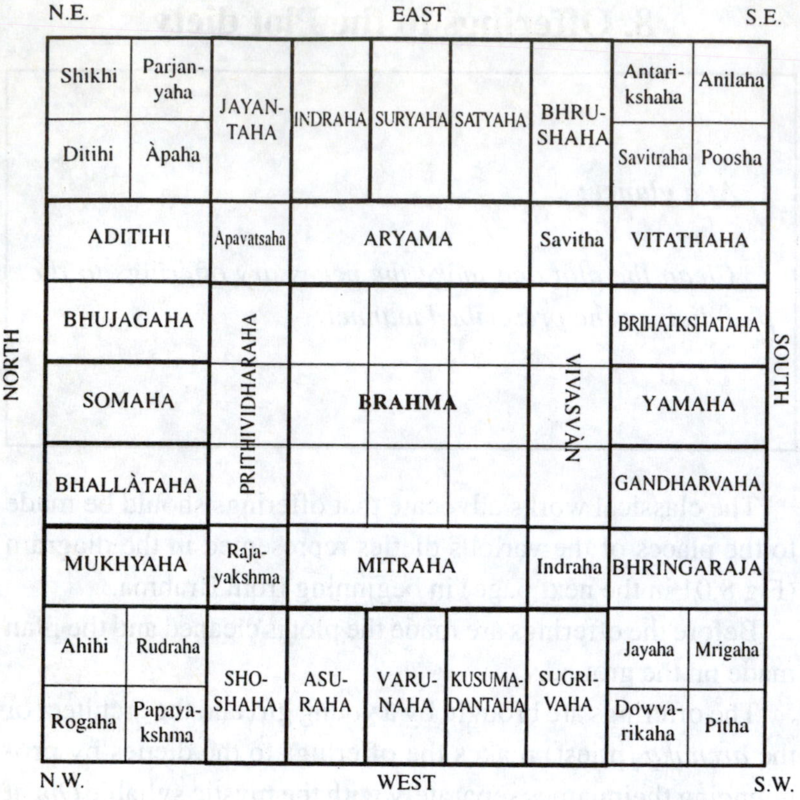
N.E.
EAST
S.E.
Shikhi
Parjan-
yaha
JAYAN-
TAHA
INDRAHA
SURYAHA
SATYAHA
BHRU-
SHAHA
Antari-
kshaha
Anilaha
Ditihi
Àpaha
Savitraha
Poosha
ADITIHI
Apavatsaha
ARYAMA
Savitha
VITATHAHA
NORTH
BHUJAGAHA
PRITHIVIDHARAHA
VIVASVÀN
BRIHATKSHATAHA
SOUTH
SOMAHA
BRAHMA
YAMAHA
BHALLÀTAHA
GANDHARVAHA
MUKHYAHA
Raja-
yakshma
MITRAHA
Indraha
BHRINGARAJA
Ahihi
Rudraha
SHO-
SHAHA
ASU-
RAHA
VARU-
NAHA
KUSUMA-
DANTAHA
SUGRI-
VAHA
Jayaha
Mrigaha
Rogaha
Papaya-
kshma
Dowva-
rikaha
Pitha
N.W.
WEST
S.W.

Fig 8.01

9. System of measurement

At a glance:

The angula and Hasta are the main units of measurement. Six types of measurement are mentioned.

The ancients used the angula (3/4") for the measurement of idols and the Hasta (24 angulas or 18") or cubit for measuring the residential buildings, temples and palaces. The Hasta was also used to measure conveyances (yana), couches (sayana), etc.

Six types of measurements are described.

Maana	—	Measurement of height or length
Pramaana	—	Measurement of breadth
Parimaana	—	Measurement of width or circumference
Lambamaana	—	Measurement along plumblines
Unmana	—	Measurement of thickness
Upamana	—	Measurement of inter space.

The Classical works also speak of the Ghanamana (exterior measurement) and Aghanamana (interior measurement)

Mana is also used generally to mean measurement.

We also have adimana which means primary measurement or comparative measurement.

Talamana is the sculptural measurement. Here the length of the face from the top of the head is the unit. This length can also be taken as the distance between the tip of the middle finger and the top of the thumb of a fully stretched palm.

Manasara mentions the following:

1 paramaanu	— 1 atom
8 paramaanu	— 1 ratha dhooli (molecule)
8 ratha Dhooli	— 1 vaalagna (hair end)
8 vaalagna	— 1 liksha (nit or egg of a louse)
8 liksha	— 1 yooka (louse)
8 yooka	— 1 yava (barley corn)
8 yava	— 1 angula ($^3/_4$")
12 angula	— 1 vitasti
2 vitasti	— 1 kishku (small cubit)
25 angula	— 1 praajaapatya (1 cubit)
26 angula	— 1 dhanurmushti
4 dhanur mushti	— 1 dhanda
8 dhanda	— 1 rajju

A rajju is the standard length of a rope and works out to 26x4x8 angula or 832 angula or roughly 52 feet. A kishku cubit (24 angula - 18") also known as hasta is normally used for measuring all objects.

The 3/4" measurement for angula is as given by Sri P.K.Acharya in his "Encyclopaedia of Architecture".

However the angula is defined as the middle phalanx of the middle finger in **Mayamata** and the yava measurement (8 barley grains placed side by side) works out to 3 cms.

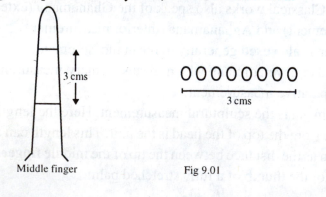

3 cms

Middle finger   Fig 9.01

3 cms

10. Ayadi Shadvarga

At a glance:

Certain formulae, called Ayadi Shadvarga are to be used in constructing a building to ensure health, wealth and prosperity for the residents.

The ancients considered the dwelling as a living organism. Whether it was a temple (**prasada**) or a palace (**rajagruha**) or a residential dwelling (**sala**) or the image (**chitra**) or idol of a deity (**vigraha**), perfection was the word that the ancients desired. They considered the plot (**kshetra**) and the dwelling (**vastu or avastha**) as having a rhythm and beauty which vibed perfectly with Nature. Each plot and building had life and there was the necessity of building the structure to perfect proportions based on certain formulae. When houses were built using these formulae, they were said to give the residents health, wealth and prosperity.

एवमायादिषड्वर्गे कुर्यात्तत्र विचक्षणौः (ण:) ॥

Evamaayadhishadvarge kuryathatra vichakshanowhu ॥

In this (matter of selecting the correct measure) the expert (architect) should apply the set of six formulae beginning with Aya (—Manasara, IX, 74)

So what are these formulae? The group of six formulae to which a structure should conform is known as Ayadi Shadvarga.

These formulae are respectively Aya, Vyaya, Rksa, Yoni, Vara and Tithi.

Ayadi Shadvarga test whether the orientation of a building is correct and whether the measurements conform to the orientation. A variety of dimensions are prescribed by the ancient treatises. These shadvarga enable the builder to select auspicious and proper dimensions of the building.

Now let us see how these formulae are calculated with specific reference to **Manasara**.

Aya (Increase)

वसुभिर्गुणितं भानु (भि) हन्यायमष्टशिष्टकम् ॥

Vasubhirgunitham Bhaanu (bhi) rhaanyaayamashta-shishtakam ॥

When the length *l* is multiplied by 8 and then divided by 12, the remainder is known as aya.

$$\frac{l \times 8}{12} \qquad [\text{remainder} = \text{aya}]$$

The results attributed to the remainder are as follows:

Remainder	Result
1	Becomes poor
2	Ill health to wife
3	Attraction of fortunes
4	Victorius
5	Sudden surprises (pleasant)
6	Righteous desires becomes fruitful
7	Becomes spiritually inclined
8	Enjoys the good things of life
9	Acquires much wealth
10	Abundance of good
11	Name and Fame

Table 10.01

If the remainder is zero, it is considered good for religious merits.

We find that except for the remainders 1 and 2, the rest indicate positive results.

Vyaya (Decrease)

नवभिर्वर्धयेत्पङ्क्तिः (त्या) हृत्वा शेषं व्ययं (यो) भवेत् ॥

Navabhirvardhayet panktihi (tya) hritvaa sesham vyayam (yo) Bhavet ॥

When the breadth (*b*) is multiplied by 9 and is divided by 10, the remainder is known as vyaya.

$$\frac{b \times 9}{10} \quad [\text{remainder} = \text{vyaya}]$$

The results are as below.

Remainder	Result
1	Achieves Success
2	Will be victorius
3	Moderate
4	Enjoys the good things of life
5	Victorius over enemies
6	Problems of the eye
7	Acquires wealth
8	Is happy (contented?) always
9	Has good friends

Table 10.02

If the remainder is zero, it is conducive to happiness.

If the aya is greater than the vyaya it is good for all round prosperity. If the aya is less than the vyaya it is said to be not auspicious. If the aya is equal to vyaya it is said to have no defect.

Rksa (Nakshatra)

अष्टाभिर्वर्धिते ऋक्षं हत्वा शेषं क्षपिष्यते ।

$$\frac{l \times 8}{27} \quad \text{[remainder = rksa]}$$

Multiply the length (*l*) by 8 and divide by 27. The remainder is called rksa or nakshatra. The odd rkshas are said to be auspicious and the even, inauspicious.

[There is some ambiguity since chapter LXIV of **Manasara** refers to the 2nd, 4th and the 9th and also the birth star under which one is born as auspicious.]

Readers will do well to refer to chapter III of Dr. B. V. Raman's **Muhurtha** for finding out the compatibility of the nakshatra of the builder with the nakshatra of the master.

Yoni (Source)

गुणनागं च योनि (निः) स्याद्वृद्धिहान्या (नयौ) यथाक्रमम् ।

Gunanaagam cha yonihi syadvriddhihaanya yathakramam।

When the breadth (*b*) is multiplied by 3 and divided by 8, the remainder is known as yoni.

$$\frac{b \times 3}{8} \quad \text{[remainder = yoni]}$$

The results are as given in the yoni Table (Fig.10.03) on the next page.

Yoni Table

Remainder	Yoni	Building to face
1	Dhwaja	East
2	Dhuma	South-east
3	Simha	South
4	Shwana	South-west
5	Vrishabha	West
6	Khara (Gandharva)	North-west
7	Gaja	North
8 (zero)	Kaaka	North-east

Table 10.03

Odd remainders are said to be auspicious and even remainders, bad. If there is no remainder the breadth has to be altered.

The yoni which is said to be an architectural formula has been given much importance by our ancients. The remainder gained through it assures the fitness of the building and the well being of the master and his surroundings. A proper yoni will ensure the qualitative life of a structure.

Brihat Samhita calculates the yoni in a slightly different manner. The area (length x breadth) is divided by 8.

The auspicious yoni defines the correct orientation of the building.

From the Yoni table above it is clear that the ancients wanted the buildings to face the four cardinal directions only viz., East, West, North and South.

The classical texts opine that Dhwaja Yoni is the best of all auspicious Yonis.

Manusyalaya Chandrika states that

Yoni constitutes the life and breath of a structure particularly of a house.

योनिः प्राणा एव धाम्नां यदस्माद् ।
ग्राह्यस्तत्तद्योग्ययोनिप्रभेदः ॥

Yonihi Praanaa Eva Dhamnam Yadasmaad |
Grahyastatadyogyayoniprabhedaha ||

Vara (Solar day)

नन्दवृद्धया ऋषिं (षिणा) हत्वा तच्छेषं वारमेव च ।

Nandavriddhayaa rishim (shina) hritva tacchesham vaarameva cha |

When the circumference is multiplied by nine and then divided by seven, the remainder is Vara.

$$\frac{c \times 9}{7} \quad [\text{remainder = vara}]$$

Multiply the circumference (c) by 9 and divide by 7. The remainder got is the Vara (solar day).

Manasara refers to C as *circumference* or *thickness* or *height*. Perhaps we can take this as the height. I invite scholars to throw more light on this point.

Remainder	Day of the Week	Result
1	Sunday	Not Favourable
2	Monday	Favourable
3	Tuesday	Not Favourable
4	Wednesday	Favourable
5	Thursday	Favourable
6	Friday	Favourable
7 (zero)	Saturday	Not Favourable

Table 10.04

Of the weekdays, Monday, Wednesday, Thursday and Friday are said to be auspicious for beginning the construction.

Tithi (lunar day)

नवभिर्गुणिते त्रिंशत् (ता) क्षपेच्छेषं तिथिर्भवेत् ।

Navabhirgunithe trimshata kshepecchesham tithirbhavet |

When the circumference is multiplied by 9 and then divided by 30, the remainder is Tithi.

$$\frac{c \times 9}{30} \quad [\text{remainder} = \text{tithi}]$$

Multiply the circumference (height) by 9 and divide by 30. The remainder indicates the Tithi (lunar day).

Remainder	Lunar Day	Results
1	Prathama	Not favourable
2	Dvitiya	Favourable
3	Tritiya	Favourable
4	Chaturthi	Not favourable
5	Panchami	Favourable
6	Sashti	Moderate
7	Saptami	Favourable
8	Ashtami	Not favourable
9	Navami	Not favourable
10	Dasami	Favourable
11	Ekadasi	Not favourable
12	Dvadasi	Favourable
13	Trayodasi	Favourable
14	Chaturdasi	Not favourable
15	Amavasya*	Not favourable

Table 10.05

* Manasara does not consider Pournima as unfavourable.

This formula gives the lunar day on which to commence the construction.

Practical Example

Let us consider a building (not a site) of length 40 hasta (or cubit), breadth 27 hasta and height 13 hasta.

Aya

$$\frac{l \times 8}{12} = \frac{40 \times 8}{12} = \frac{320}{12} \qquad \text{[Remainder = 8]}$$

Vyaya

$$\frac{b \times 9}{10} = \frac{29 \times 9}{10} = \frac{243}{10} \qquad \text{[Remainder = 3]}$$

Rksa

$$\frac{l \times 8}{27} = \frac{40 \times 8}{27} = \frac{320}{27} \qquad \text{[Remainder = 23]}$$

Yoni

$$\frac{b \times 3}{8} = \frac{27 \times 3}{8} = \frac{81}{8} \qquad \text{[Remainder = 1]}$$

Vara

$$\frac{c \times 9}{7} = \frac{8 \times 9}{7} = \frac{72}{7} \qquad \text{[Remainder = 2]}$$

Tithi

$$\frac{h \times 9}{30} = \frac{8 \times 9}{30} = \frac{72}{30} \qquad \text{[Remainder = 12]}$$

Summarising the shadvarga of the building and its consequent results are as in Table 10.06 of next page:

Aya	=	8	Vyaya	=	3
Riskha	=	23	Yoni	=	1
Vara	=	2	Tithi	=	12

Table 10.06

For the building under reference:

Aya is 8 — Enjoys the good things of life.

Vyaya is 3 — Moderate

Since Aya is greater than Vyaya, all round prosperity is indicated.

Rksa is 23, odd, and so favourable.

Yoni is 1, Dhwaja, and is the best of all Yonis. The building has to face East.

Vara is 2 indicating Monday and therefore good. Construction can begin on this day.

Tithi is 12 or the 12th day (Dwadasi) and hence favourable.

Reference to **Vayas** or age of the building is also made to in certain texts.

The remainder obtained by multiplying the area of the building (l x b) by 27 and dividing by 100 is the **Vayas** or age of the building.

In the example worked above, the age of the building will be 60 years.

$$\frac{(40 \times 27) \times 27}{100} = \frac{29160}{100}$$

Remainder is 60 which is **Vayas** or **age** of the building.

Of all the Shadvarga Aya, Vyaya, Yoni and Nakshatra are extremely important. If the measurement of the building conforms to these four formulae, we can assume that the structure more or less is proportionate.

Manasara recommends 9 different lengths, 9 different breadths and 5 different heights. Of these different and varying measures, the right measure is selected by applying the 6 formulae. By a verification of the measurements with the respective formula, the risk of selecting improper measurements will be eliminated. The ancient structures which conformed to these Ayadi are even today standing strong and tall.

The following slokas from **Manasara** (Ch.LXIV, 85-87) are appropriate.

यत्र दोषो गुणाधिक्यं तत्र .दोषो न विद्यते ।

तेषामधिकगुणां वानं (न्यं) सर्वदोषकरं भवत् ॥

तस्मात्परिहरेद् विद्वान् जनमेवं प्रकल्पयेत् ।

Where there is more worth than flaw, there is no defect in it, but if the worth is more than the flaw, it would be imperfect; therefore, the knowledgeable (architect) should avoid the calculation that is imperfect and follow the practice that is current among the people.

11. Brahmasthana

At a glance:

The Brahmasthana (the central square of the plot) is an important factor to be reckoned while constructing a building. The energy lines running through the centre of the plot are also equally important.

In ancient times villages, towns, temples (**Prasada**), palaces (**Rajagriha**) and even dwelling places (**Sala**) were constructed in such a manner that the central portions either contained a temple, deity, courtyard or in the case of a village or town a huge central hall for the assembly of people.

The central portion called the Brahmasthana corresponds to the nine squares of the 81 grid plan (also called the **paramasayika padavinyasa**). The Brahmasthana is the region round the navel (**Nabhi**) of the Vastu Purusha (plot deity).

Brihat Samhita says:

सुखमिच्छन् ब्रह्माणां यत्नाद्रक्षेद्गृही गृहान्तःस्थम्
उच्छिष्टाद्युपताद् गृहपतिरूपतप्यते तस्मिन् ॥

— Chp LIII, SI 66

*A house-owner (**Yajamana**) who wants happiness should guard very carefully Brahman (the central nine squares). Affliction in this area by way of dirty things like leftovers would harm the owner in it.*

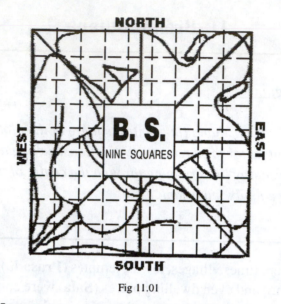

Fig 11.01

The **Manasara** categorically states that in the Brahmasthana, the temple of the family deity can be built.

The ancients also talked about certain lines running across a plot crossing the Brahmasthana. As these lines corresponded to several body parts of the *Vastu Purusha*, they concluded that much care was to be taken in building a structure, so that these parts were not 'hurt'. The points at which these lines cut the Brahmasthana were also to be guarded carefully.

In fact, **Mayamata** also talks about vulnerable points and calls them *Marma*. These are the lines joining the north with south and the east with west. The north-south line is called *Nadi* and the east-west line *Vamsa*. The diagonals running across the Brahmasthana are called *Konasutra*. These are highly sensitive energy lines.

The **Brihat Samhita** also talks about these vulnerable points. It states that the meeting points of the longer diagonals and the exact middle points of the squares have to be considered as vulnerable points which ought not to be hurt.

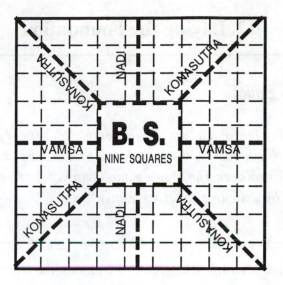

Fig 11.02

The following sloka from **Brihat Samhita** is interesting (Ch.LIII, Sloka 58)

तान्यशुचिभाण्डकीलस्तम्भादैः पीडितानि शल्यैश्च ।
गृह्भर्तुस्तत्तुल्ये पीडामङ्गे प्रयच्छन्ति ॥

meaning broadly, if these, vulnerable points are 'hurt' by nails, pillars, pegs, heavy objects, the owner will be troubled in the corresponding limbs of his body.

It becomes clear that the Brahmasthana and the energy lines have to be safeguarded.

12. Laying the Foundation

At a glance:

Laying the foundation should begin after proper prayers in the North-east. A good muhurtha should be set by an expert astrologer. The digging and laying of the foundation should be done in a precise manner.

After the offerings are given to the dieties, the Guddali pooja or Bhumi pooja should be done in the North-east corner of the plot. The first digging should be done either by the master and/or the architect (sthapathi) or the chief mason (vardhaki) at an auspicious time (muhurtha) set by a learned astrologer. Before digging begins appropriate pooja should be performed in the North-east corner of the plot by a learned purohit facing the East.

Astrologically, the auspicious lunar months are: 1. Chaitra 2. Vaisakha 3. Sravana 4. Kartika 5. Magha. The Sun should preferably occupy a fixed sign.

For laying the foundation the following constellations are recommended:

1. Rohini;   2. Mrigasira;   3. Hasta;   4. Chitta;
5. Uttara;   6. Jyeshta;   7. Uttarashada; 8. Sravana.

All odd lunar days except the 9th are good. The 2nd, 6th and 10th lunar days are also auspicious. Of the weekdays Wednesday, Thursday and Friday are recommended.

The rising sign or lagna should be a fixed sign. The lagna should be strengthened by the presence of malefics in 3rd, 6th and 11th houses and benefics in Kendra (quadrants) and trikonas (trines). The eighth house should be vacant without the aspect of a malefic planet.

The Adhika Masa as a 'rule' may be avoided. Construction activity should not be started if any female member of the family is in her 6th month of pregnancy or if any member is seriously ill.

Digging of the soil for laying the foundation should be in the following order.

1. North-east Sector
2. North-west Sector
3. South-east Sector
4. South-west Sector

The diagram below explains this better

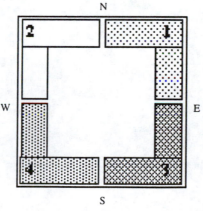

Fig 12.01

Laying of the Foundation should be in the reverse of the above viz.,

1. South-west
2. South-east
3. North-west
4. North-east

The diagram below explains the previous page.

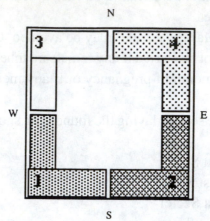

Fig 12.02

13. Digging the Well

At a glance:

A well should be dug as soon as the pooja is performed. A well (or sump) should preferably be placed in the North of North-east. Deep wells are good.

As soon as a site is selected and the appropriate poojas are performed, the first thing that you have to do is to dig a well or sump.

The marking of the plot and building should be done. If the water diviner finds that the water is available either in the north or noth east of the site, a well may be dug. Else it is better to settle for a sump.

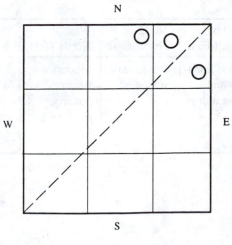

Fig 13.01

Care should be taken to dig the well or sump in such a manner that the energy lines do not cross the well or sump. The following diagram may be referred.

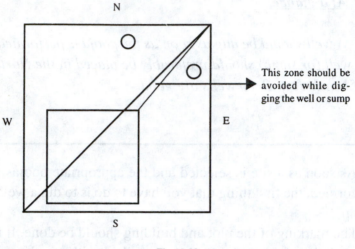

This zone should be avoided while digging the well or sump

Fig 13.02

The following table gives the likely results for the various placements of the well or sump.

Well dug in	East of North-East	North of North-East	West of North-West	North of North-West
Results	Good finances and education.	Increase of finances, and prosperity.	Moderate finances, poverty, bitterness in family.	Litigation, quarrels over finances.

Table 17.01

Well dug in	South/West of South-West	South/East of South-East	Brahmasthana or Centre of Plot
Results	Death of eldest member or head of family goes financially or otherwise broke, quarrels with or among women.	Problems to and from children. Finances crumble and no cordiality in the family, danger from fire.	Disintegration of family

Table 13.02

The **Brihat Samhita**, however recommends wells or sumps in north and north east only.

Brihat Samhita

Well in	Results
East	Loss of children
South east	Danger from fire
South	Fear of enemies
South west	Quarrels among women
West	Weakness of women in the family
North west	Poverty
North	Increase of wealth
North east	Prosperity of children

Table 13.03

If you observe the pushkarinis of temples doing well, you will notice that most of them are to the north of north-east.

You will also find that these are not only very wide in the shape of a square but also fairly deep. I feel that this principle should be followed, especially while constructing sumps —

be squares and go as deep as possible.

You can also have your sumps in proportion to the site dimensions. For example for a 40' x 60' site have your sumpdug in 2:3 ratio with the depth either 2 or 3 depending on your requirement of water.

This will enhance the benefits of vastu for the residents.

The following table as given in **Mayamata** is also self-explanatory.

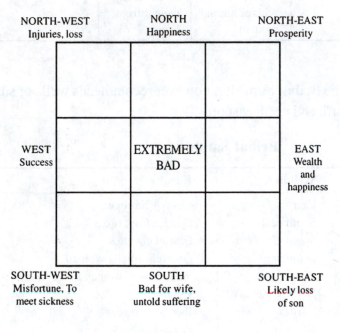

Fig 13.03

14. Compound Walls

At a glance:

All the four sides of a building should have a compound well. Gates have to be provided at specified places.

The compound walls must be constructed next. Depending on the road the gates can be provided as per the following table.

Road in	Gates to be in
North	4th part of nine parts from west
West	4th part of nine parts from south
South	4th part of nine parts from east
East	4th part of nine parts from north

Table 14.01

The diagrams (Fig 14.01) on the next page explain the placements of the gates better.

The compounds have to be perfectly oriented to the directions. Make use of a compass or sankhu to first fix the directions, then put pegs beginning from north-east, north-west, south-east and then south-west corners. Tie the pegs with a cord and then construct the walls.

Always have your compound walls on the south and west higher and thicker than the north and east walls. Depending on security factors you can study the possibility of having on the

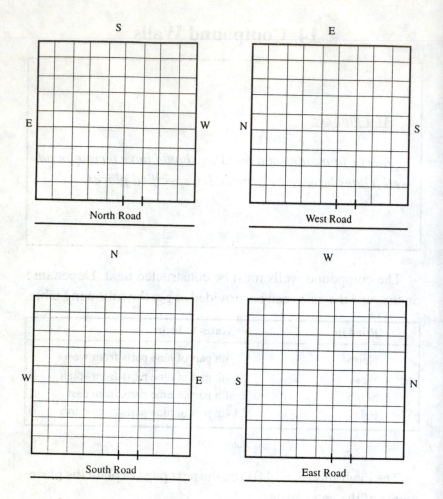

Fig 14.01

north and east sides a fencing instead of a wall. This will ensure that the plot is flooded with the positive energies from the Sun.

Stone walls on the South and West and brick walls on the North and East may also be thought of.

The building to come up later may be totally independent of the compound walls.

The space to be left between the building and the compound wall should be atleast 1/9 of the length and breadth of the site.

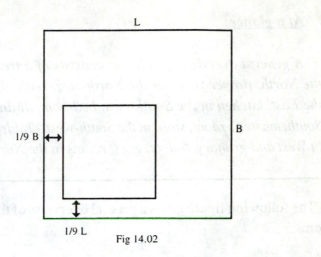

Fig 14.02

If a garage has to come it can be either in the north-west or in the south-east touching the compound wall but not the main building.

15. House

At a glance:

A general overview of a house consists of a treasury in the North, prayer room in the North-east, bath, dining in the East, kitchen in the South-east, bedroom, dining in the South, master's room, store in the South-west, children room in West and granary, toilets, guest rooms in the North west.

The following figure gives a general overview of the various rooms.

NORTH-WEST (VAYUVYA)	NORTH (UTTARA)	NORTH-EAST (EASHANYA)	
Granary, Toilets, Animal Sheds, Garage, Guest Rooms	Treasury	Pooja, Verandah, Portico, No weights	
Children Study Room	Court-yard	Bath, Dining, Store for fluids like Ghee, milk	EAST (POORVA)
Master Bed Room, Dressing Room, Store for assets	Bed Room, Dining	Kitchen, Garage	
SOUTH-WEST (NIRUTI)	SOUTH (DAKSHINA)	SOUTH-EAST (AGNEYA)	

WEST (PASCHIMA)

Fig 15.01

It is adviseable to have the structure or building constructed in south-west portion of the plot. More space on the north and east may be allowed.

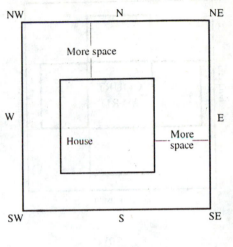

Fig 15.02

The classical works recommend the *paisacha* zone to be kept free.

Fig 15.03

The ancients speak of four types of houses.

Ekasala: Courtyard surrounded by chambers on one side.

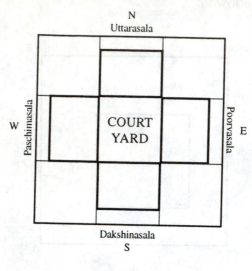

Fig 15.03

Dwisala: Courtyard surrounded by chambers on two sides.

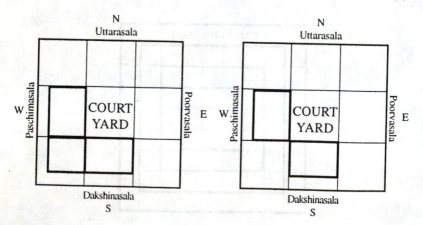

Fig 15.04

Trisala: Courtyard surrounded by chambers on three sides.

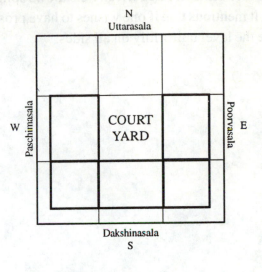

Fig 15.05

Chatussala: Courtyard surrounded by chambers on all four sides.

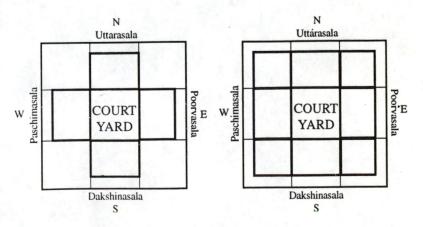

Fig 15.06

I propose to go into details of these houses in my next book.

The **Brihat Samhita** categorically disallows split level constructions. It mentions that if one wishes to have prosperity, one has to raise the level uniformly on all sides.

16. The Mahadwara (Main door)

At a glance:

The placement of the main door is very important. The four important zones for placing a main door beginning from East are 1)Indra 2)Brhatakshata 3)Kusumadanta and 4)Bhallata respectively. Avoid doors in the middle of a building.

We have to first decide on the placement of the main door (*Mahadwara* or *Mooladwara*). The following diagrams shows the most favourable or exalted positions for the main door. Each side of the house is divided into nine parts.

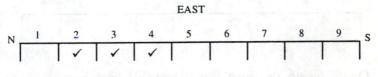

Fig 16.01

On the east, the second, third and fourth parts which are assigned to *Parjanya, Jayanta* and *Indra* respectively are the exalted zones. The results attributed by **Brihat Samhita** are:

Parjanya : Birth of daughters
Jayanta : Financial soundness
Indra   : Royal favour

Fig 16.02

On the South, the fourth part assigned to *Brihatakshata* is the exalted zone.

Result attributed by **Brihat Samhita** is increase of food and children.

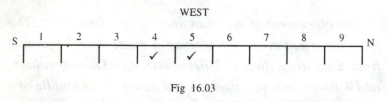

Fig 16.03

On the West, the exalted zones are the fourth and fifth parts corresponding to the *Kusumadanta* and *Varuna* respectively.

Brihat Samhita attributes the following results.

Kusumadanta : Prosperity of sons and increase of wealth.

Varuna   : Increase of wealth.

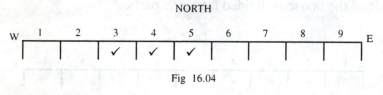

Fig 16.04

On the North, the third, fourth and fifth parts represented by *Mukhya, Bhallata* and *Soma* respectively are said to be ideal for main doors.

Brihat Samhita attributes the following results:

Mukhya : Increase of wealth and birth of sons.

Bhallata : Possession of all virtues.

Soma   : Begetting of children and wealth.

Ideally the main building can have door on all the four sides in the fourth exalted zone. In fact **Mayamata** and **Samarangana Sutradhara** specifically recommends the placement of the door in the *Mahendra (Indra), Brihatakshata, Kusumadanta* and *Bhallata*.

The consolidated diagram below shows the recommended position of the main door.

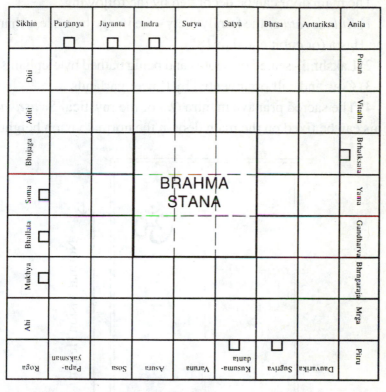

Fig 16.05

As we can see from the above, the ancients never placed the main door by whim and fancy.

The main door can be the biggest of all doors. **Manasára** suggests that the height of a door has to be atleast twice its width. **Brihat Samhita** and **Visvakarma Prakasha** prescribe a height thrice the width of the door.

The main door has to be attractive, solid and massive. **Mayamata** suggests that the main door can be strengthened with the help of various metals.

How wonderful that the ancients foresaw the need for solid security in the 21st century!

The main door can be decorated by the following:

1) *Kuladevata* or the family diety - the image being less than one Hasta (or cubit equal to 18")

2) Lakshmi - seated on a lotus and being bathed by elephants.

3) Cow and calf ornamented by flower garlands.

4) The sacred pranava mantra *Om* or the mystical *Swastika*. This can be fixed on the main door at the normal vision height.

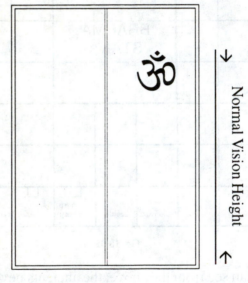

Fig 16.06

It is always advisable to have a sill or threshold not only for the main door but also the other doors. The reason could be that the threshold acts as a block for insects, etc. coming from the outside. The threshold can perhaps also regulate the powerful ground energies into the building and its various rooms.

The **Samarangana Sutradhara** does not recommend more than five *shakas* (frames) for a door.

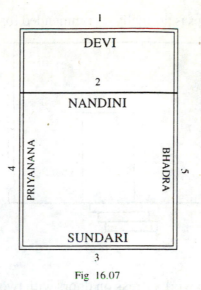

Fig 16.07

The total frame can include the fifth horizontal frame (Nandini to give us a ventilator at the top of the door.

A main door in the middle of the house is normally not rec-ommended.

The following sloka from **Samarangana Sutradhara** is an eye opener.

मध्ये द्वारं न कर्तव्यं मनुजानां कथञ्चन ।
मध्ये द्वारे कृते तत्र कुलनाशः प्रजायते ॥

which broadly translated means, that a door in the middle indicates ruin of the family.

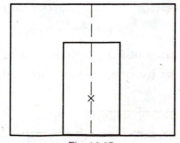

Fig 16.07

A flight of steps is normally recommended for the main door.

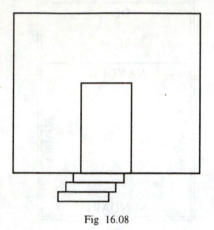

Fig 16.08

Most classical works stress on doors with two (leaves) shutters but do not prohibit doors with single leaves.

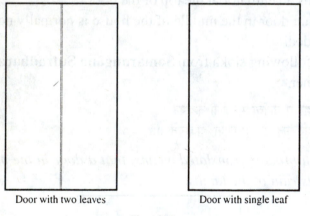

Door with two leaves   Door with single leaf

Fig 16.09

Manasara recommends the right leaf to be wider in breadth and the left leaf less by one, two or three angulas ($3/_4$", $1^1/_2$", $2^1/_4$")

दक्षिणस्य कवाटं तु विशालाधिकमायतम् ।
एकद्वित्र्यडलं वामकवाटं स्याद् द्विहस्त (विहीन) कम् ॥

SECTION II

1. Master Bedroom

At a glance:

The South west sector is for the master's room. Sleep with your head to the south. Outside the master room, a rock garden can be made. This will provide a natural setting as you look out from the window.

The master bedroom can be in the south-west of the building. This room may be occupied by the father or the eldest son of the family. The beds or cots can be away from the walls but may be towards the south-west corner of the room.(1) Master cupboards to contain valuable documents, cash, jewellery etc. should be in the South-west of the room such that the cupboard

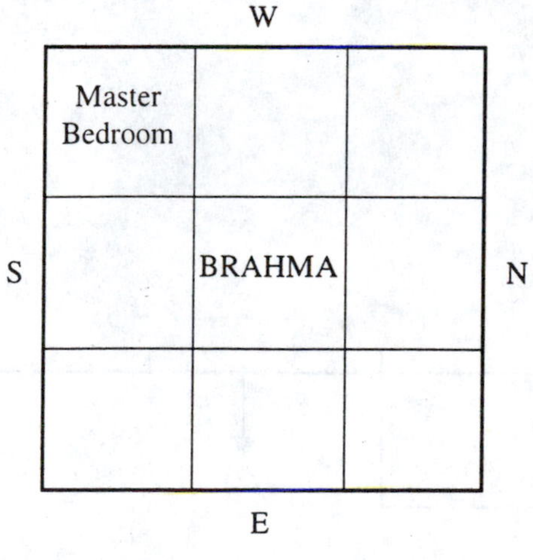

Fig B1.01

opens to the north or the region of Kubera.(2) The North room of the house can also be used to store valuables, property papers, cash , jewellery, etc. Cupboards for clothes can be in the north-west.(3) It is adviseable to have a north or east door for a master bedroom.(4)

The dressing table can be in east or north of the room.(5) If you wish to have an attached toilet, let it be to the north-west or south-east of the room.(6)

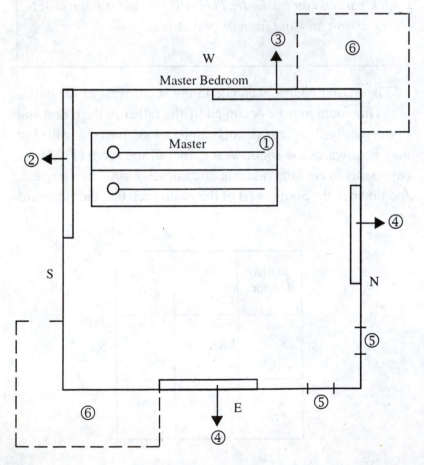

Fig B1.02

2. The Bathroom

At a glance:

The East sector is best suited for a bathroom since the beneficial rays of the morning sun fall into the room. Go in for stone flooring.

Manasara says : The Aditi block (meaning the true east) is the place for bathrooms. The bathroom, where one has his daily

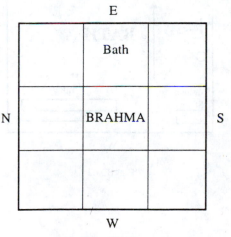

Fig B2.01

bath is best in the east, as recommended by the ancients. The morning rays of the Sun are said to be extremely beneficial. Hence proper windows (of course with due provision for privacy) may be provided on the east wall of the bath room. The slopes within the bathroom can be towards north and east so

that water drains into the north-east of the bathroom. The gey-
ser or the boiler can be in the South-east of the bathroom. Mirrors can be on the east and north walls. Taps and shower can be
in north so that the water drains to the north-east. Bath tub can
be on the west side with head towards south. Avoid a door on
the south-west of the bathroom. Washing stone if required can
be provided in the north-west. Go in for stone flooring to keep
children and yourself from slipping and falling in the bathroom.

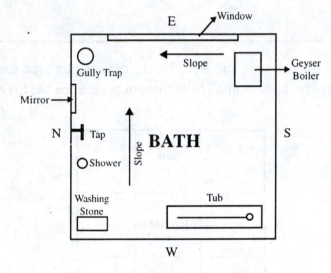

Fig B2.02

3. Children's (study) Rooms

__At a glance:__

Children's room can be in the west or north sector. Let them sleep with their heads to the west.

Children's rooms can be in the west or north of the building. They can have their beds to the south-west corner of the room with heads on the west. Of course let not the beds (or cots) touch the walls. They can have their desks on the east or north and face east while studying. The rooms can have an east or north door. A green bulb will be effective in enhancing the intelligence of the child.

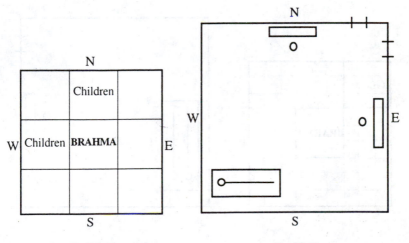

Fig B3.01   Fig B3.02

4. Guest Rooms

At a glance:

Reserve the North-west for guest rooms. Avoid children in this room.

North-west rooms are ideal for guests and newly weds. The cot/s can be in the south-west of the room without touching the walls and with the head towards south. The table can be on the east wall. As the diety ruling north-west is Vayu or the wind-god, it is best to avoid children, especially in their formative years to occupy a North-west room.

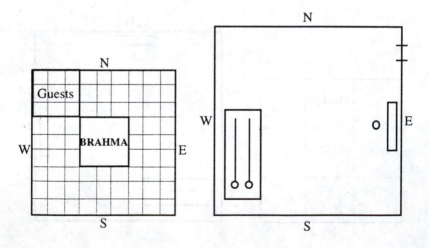

Fig B4.01   Fig B4.02

5. Kitchen

At a glance:

The right place for kitchen is the South-east sector. Face the east while cooking. The gas stove can be in the South east corner of the Kitchen.

South-east portion of the building is the place for your kitchen. Even though some authors permit the north-west, the writer feels that as south-east is ruled by Agni or the fire-god, the south-east kitchen is best.

The kitchen can have an east platform for cooking. The gas stove or burner can be placed to the corner such that the lady of the house does the cooking facing east towards the south corner. Try to have the platform stand on supports so that it does not touch the east and South walls. The sink for washing can be in the north-east corner of the kitchen. Big windows and ventilators can be provided on the east and smaller windows on the south. The exhaust fan can be on the eastern wall towards the south-east corner. Have the kitchen door either in the north of north-east or west of north-west.

Lofts and almirahs can be on the south and west sides.

To stimulate appetite have your kitchen walls painted soft pink or orange.

As good food is indicative of financial strength, a mirror on the eastern wall will likely help strengthen finances.

Drinking water can be placed in the north-east, brooms and

cleaning materials in the north-west and stocks of rice, dal and other heavy materials can be kept in the south-west of the kitchen.

In case the south-east kitchen is not possible, you can do with the north-west of the building. But make sure that the observations made above for the south-east kitchen are followed.

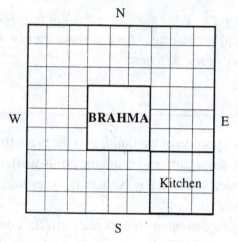

Fig B5.01

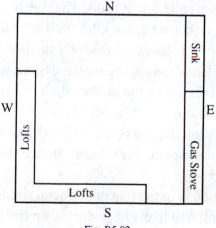

Fig B5.02

6. Dining Room

At a glance:

West or East rooms are for the dining hall. Stimulate the appetite by having walls painted soft pink or orange.

The suggested place is west. However the writer feels it is wise to have the dining room in the east as it would be near the kitchen if placed in south-east. However if the kitchen is in the north-west, you can comfortably settle for a west dining room.

The dining table, preferably a rectangular one should be so arranged that the master of the house, or his wife or eldest son occupies the south of south-west or west of south-west chair in the room. Odd shapes like egg shaped or other irregular shapes are best avoided for dining tables. The dining table should be away from the walls. The fridge can occupy the south-east of the room

If a wash basin has to be placed, it can be in the north or east of the room with the water draining to the north-east corner.

The dining room can either be an independent room or a continuation of the kitchen.

The dining room should serve the intended purpose. Family members who dine here should eat well to their heart's content. Appetite can be stimulated by painting the walls soft pink or orange or cream and by installing a mirror on the east and/or north wall.

Wall paintings depicting the rising Sun, and the beauty of nature (without its wild inhabitants) will create an ambience of happiness.

Let the dining room be a haven for the family members.

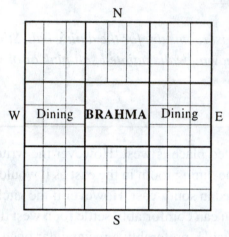

Fig B6.01

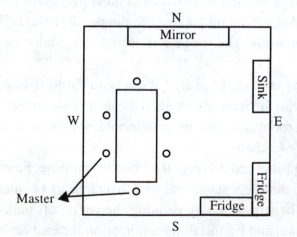

Fig B6.02

7. Living Room

At a glance:

Living Rooms can be in the North-east sector. Avoid loads in the centre of the hall.

These can be the north, east or north-east sector of the building. Depending on the road, living room can be manipulated. However it is to be noted that the inner walls of the living room do not fall on the konasutras described elsewhere in the earlier pages.

As far as possible have an east of north-east door. If the living room happens to be the direct entry into the house, construct it in such a way that it is more spacious to your right as you enter it. This is necessary since the first impression one gets on entering is one of spaciousness. The living area can be strengthened by having wall sceneries, flower pots and spot lights at strategic places.

The furniture can be placed in the south and west allowing good space on the north and east.

The master can occupy the south-west corner sofa facing either the east or the north.

Sceneries and mirrors, if required can be on the north and east walls.

Heavy indoor plants can be strategically placed on the south or West of the living room.

Diwanas or sitting beds (or light furniture) can be in the east and north areas.

The north-east of the room can have a diety's photo.

White, soft blue and soft green are the colours recommended.

Avoid heaviness in the centre of the living room.

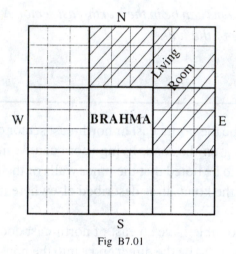

Fig B7.01

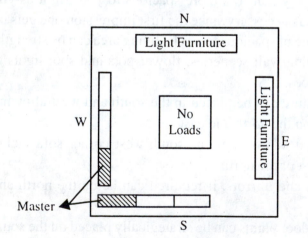

Fig B7.02

8. Prayer Rooms

At a glance:

Prayer rooms can be either in the North-east sector or the Brahmasthana of a house. Let the diety be on the eastern side. Pyramid shaped roofs assist in meditation.

Depending on the size of the plot or the nature of the building the prayer room can either be in the north-east sector or.in the Brahmasthana.

1. For normal houses, the north-east is the best position. It can also be slightly to the east or north.

Let the diety be on the east wall so that we face the rising sun while paying obeisance to the deity.

To enhance the intended purpose of the room, *viz.*, spirituality, communion with the Almighty and meditation, a pyramid roof is recommended. The following types are all fine.

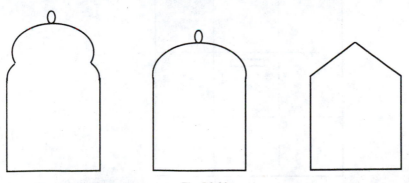

Fig B8.01

Great spiritual energy is said to flow from the tip of the pyramid into the room. A person doing prayer is immensely benefitted. It is also said that a pyramid has healing properties. An ill person can certainly benefit by sitting in such a prayer room for about 30 minutes a day, facing east or north.

White or soft shades of blue are recommended.

There can be a big east window above the diety to let in the morning rays of the sun. All cupboards in the prayer room can be in the south and west walls.

Avoid having photos of dead people along with the photos of your diety.

Unless you have tremendous spiritual control and capable of doing pujas everyday in a systematic manner, avoid having Srichakra, Saligramas and idols of ancient temples in the puja room.

Keep the puja room absolutely clean.

If you are forced to have your puja in the kitchen, have your diety in the North-east of the kitchen, facing west.

Never have the puja room in the bedroom.

If it is a very big plot the puja room can be constructed in the centre of the plot or centre of the building. The diety can be placed in such a way that you face East while worshipping it.

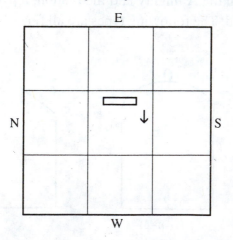

Fig B8.02

Similarly this concept can be adopted while planning a shrine for an industry or a factory or a group of houses or flats. The north east sector of course can also have your private shrine.

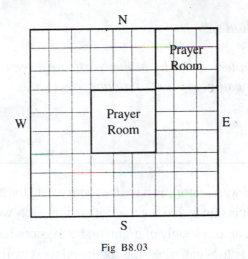

Fig B8.03

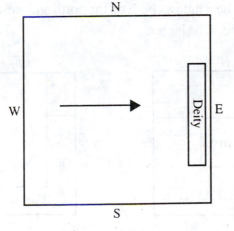

Fig B8.04

9. Store Rooms

At a glance:

The granaries can be in the North-west sector. Lofts and attics can be on the South and West walls.

The north-west sector can have the room meant for storing grains, provisions. It is said by having the store in the north-west there will always be a copious supply of grains and provisions into the house! The lofts and attics can be on the south and west walls.

Oil, butter, milk, etc. can be kept in the south-east of the room. Heavy provisions can be stored in the south-west of the room. Grains that are needed for daily use can be in the north-west corner.

There can be windows both on the north and west walls, but let those on the north be larger.

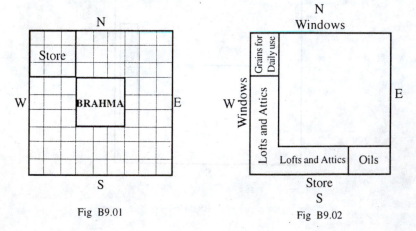

Fig B9.01   Fig B9.02

10. Toilets

At a glance:

Toilets are to be in the North-west sector. Avoid them in the centre of the building.

These again can be in the north-west Sector. The ancients had the excellent practice of having the toilets out of the main building to the corner of the plot in the north-west sector. Added to this they kept these toilets totally clear of the main building. Even today there are many houses having their toilets outside the main building. However taking due note of the security problems of today as also the limitations of space we can, if it is not possible to have it outside the building, have the toilet inside the building — in the north-west sector. The alternate place is the south-east, but avoid having the toilet either in the north-east or south-west.

As eashanya is the confluence of Kubera and Indra, it is said that toilet in the north-east will gradually weaken the finances and the general prosperity of the master of the house. Similarly toilets in the south-west make the master indecisive and his health may suffer.

Toilets in the Brahmasthana or the centre of the building are also totally prohibited.

Attached toilets can be in the north-west portion of the room. Have the bigger window on the north and a smaller one in the west after providing for privacy. Toilet seats from north to south are generally approved. Mirrors in the toilet may be on the north and east walls.

Let the walls be coloured using light shades to make your stay in the toilet comfortable!

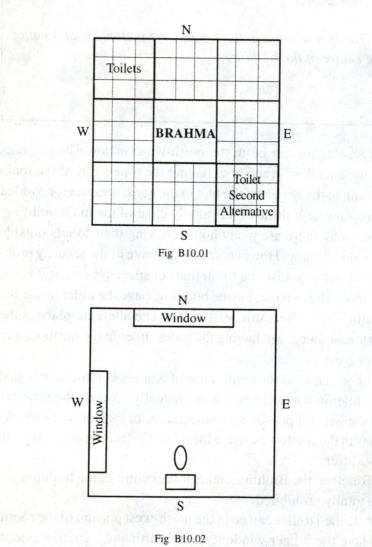

Fig B10.01

Fig B10.02

11. Rooms in general

At a glance:

South-east bedrooms may be avoided. Blue colour in-duces sleep. Green is good for study. Almirahs and lofts can be in the South or west of the rooms.

Avoid bedrooms in the south-east. A south-east bedroom if occupied by couples generally indicates constant quarrels between them over petty matters as also encourage in excessive expenditure!

Generally speaking avoid beds in the centre of the room; avoid a door in the south-west sector of the room; do not sleep with your head to the north and under beams. Get a good night's sleep by burning a true blue zero candle bulb in your room.

For a study room (childrens), have your walls painted soft green to encourage your children to concentrate. The master room and rooms for guests and couples can be painted in different hues of blue (of your liking) to give you good sleep and prevent you from consuming sleeping tablets.

Let almirahs, lofts, wardrobes be on the South and West sides of the room.

12. A note on Agni

At a glance:

Agni or Fire can be pacified by using a wick lamp or a spotlight or an electrical gadget or a mirror.

As South-east belongs to agni he can create enough trouble for the inmates! The South-east corners of every room should be taken care of. It is to be noted that if proper appeasement of Agni is not made, the following problems are likely to arise.

1. Bitterness in the family
2. Ill health to the inmates
3. Financial weakness
4. Marital discords

You can keep Agni happy by:

1. Having a spotlight or lantern or the traditional wick lamp in the South-east corner with light or burning flame pointing to the roof.

2. Having a mirror on the eastern corner of the South-east.

3. Having an electrical gadget like a television, VCR, fridge, washing machine, radio placed in the south East corner.

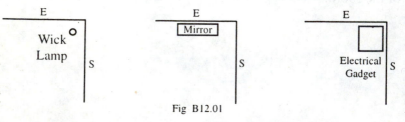

Fig B12.01

13. Septic Tanks and Garages

At a glance:

Septic tanks and garages can be in the North-west sector. A second choice for garages is the South-east. Let not the garage touch the main building.

The preferred place is north-west or vayuvya. Avoid touching the compound walls or the foundation.

Garages can be in the north-west or as a second choice in the south-east. Let the garage be a independent unit without touching the main building. If the portico is used for parking let it be on the north or east of the plot, never in north-east. Let the car face north or east, as the case may be when parked. Let the portico be one or two feet below the roof level without touching the main building. Avoid your garages or portico in south-west.

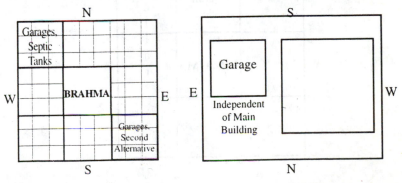

Fig B13.01   Fig B13.02

14. Basements and Cellars

At a glance:

The North, east and north east are ideal for basements. Avoid cellars in the south west.

If there is the need for a cellar, the best place is the north and east of the plot. Of course, the basement is not meant for residing. Avoid basements and cellars in the south-west. It may render the master or the eldest son weak and accidents are likely to occur in the family.

A height equal to the ground floor height is generally recommended.

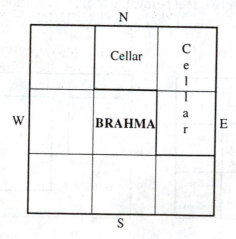

Fig B14.01

15. Staircases

At a glance:

Staircases may be anywhere except in the North east and Brahmasthana. However as much as possible prefer them in the South, West or south west sectors.

The staircase can be placed in the south, west and south-west. Avoid staircases in the north-east as they can cause problems with your finance.

The step should begin either from the north or east. The turning of the staircase has to be clockwise only. The last step should be towards south or west.

If it is an internal staircase avoid the staircase just opposite the entrance. Similarly for outside staircases avoid crossing the main door.

The space beneath the staircase should not be occupied by any one. It can be used to function like a lumbar room.

Avoid placing the staircase in the centre of the house (in the Brahmasthana).

If staircases in the north-west or south-east are mandatory, have the staircases as light as possible. However, the beginning step and ending step, and the rotation of the stairs should be as suggested above.

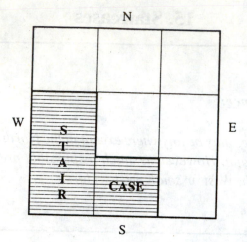

Fig 15.01

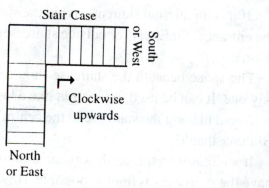

Fig 15.02

16. Overhead Water Tank

At a glance:

The overhead tank can be placed in the west of south west avoiding the **Konasutra** *running from North east to South west. Avoid having overhead tank in the middle of the building.*

Have the overhead tank placed on the west side of the south-west corner of the building. Some scholars opine that the overhead tank can be in the south-west corner. However if you observe the vastu-purusha diagram, you will conclude it is better to avoid the corner as it disturbs the konasutra. Let the tank be one or two feet from the parapet wall. The tank can be placed on a small brick platform of 9" height.

Avoid the overhead tank in the other places. The following results are generally attributed to wrong placements.

Over Head Tank in	Result
North-east	Considerable Financial and health disturbances
South-east	Severe financial crisis, accidents and litigations

Table 16.01

Generally south, north, north-west are best avoided.

Do not place the over-head tank in the middle of the structure. In such cases, it is said the building becomes an orphan! To put in simple terms, the family will somehow not be able to stay in the house permanently.

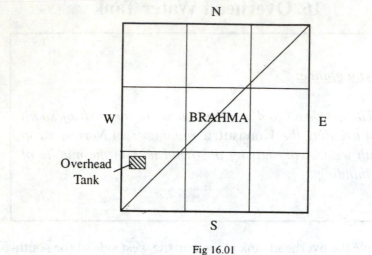

Fig 16.01

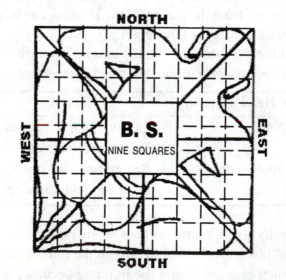

Fig 16.02

17. Levels of the Floor

At a glance:

Split levels inside the building are not recommended by the ancients.

The ancient texts do not approve of various levels in the structure itself. Brihat Samhita, for instance says that if one wishes for the prosperity of one's household, one ought to raise the level of the floor uniformly on all sides. However some scholars opine that to strengthen the niruti, the south-west rooms can be higher. The author does not subscribe to this veiw.

Uniform Level

| N | E | S | W |

Classical View

Fig 17.01

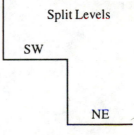

Split Levels

SW

NE

Modern View

Fig 17.02

18. Verandah or the first room into the structure

At a glance:

Verandahs can be in the East or North. Have a proper **mahadwara**.

This room is preferred in the east or north of the building. The general emphasis should be on more expanse on to your right, as you enter, than to your left. Let the east or north walls (to your left) have a mirror to reflect the spaciousness of the verandah. You can have the furniture arranged in the south and west.

Let the shoe-rack be in the north-west of the verandah. Have large windows on the north and east walls. Of course have a proper mahadwara or main door, as discussed in an earlier chapter.

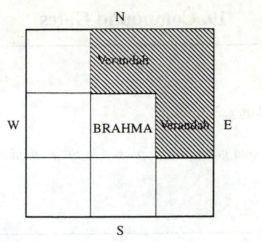

Fig 18.01

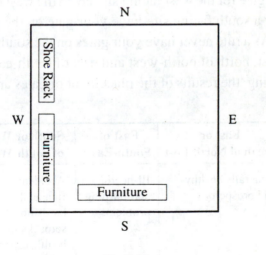

Fig 18.02

19. Compound Gates

At a glance:

Compound gates can be placed in the exalted regions.

Have your gates placed depending on the direction the plot is. For instance, the north facing site can have its gate on the north of north-east.

The East facing site can have the gate on the east of north-east. Let the gate for the west facing site be on the west of north-west. As for a south facing site have your gate on the south of south-east. As a rule never have your gates on the south or west of south-west, north of north-west and east of south-east. Generally speaking, the results of the placement of gates are as follows:

Gate in	East or North of North-East	East of South-East	South or West of South-West
Result	Generally healthy and prosperous	Ill-health and burning problems	Accidents, financial hardships and setbacks in health, especially for the master

Fig 19.01

SECTION III

1. Generally speaking . . . .

> ### *At a glance:*
>
> *Open spaces corresponding to* **paisacha** *zone are to be left alround the building. Leaf bearing trees can be grown in the South west of the compound.* **Darbhe** *grass can be grown for its healing properties in the North east portion.*

Open spaces all around the building are always good.

The zone marked paisacha in the diagram below may be avoided.

PAISÀCHA ZONE

Fig C1.01

However more open space on the north and east are recommended. It is always adviseable to have the main building independent of the compound walls.

Leaf bearing trees like ashoka, neem, guava, coconut, banana can be planted on the South and West of the building. During summer the trees prevent the hot afternoon air from directly coming into the south-west bedroom, thus keeping the room cool. During winter the same trees work as a filter and the extremely cold air gets warmed up as it enters the room thus making the room comfortable for the inmates.

Be prudent to plant the trees, especially taking care that their roots do not filter into the foundation and damage the building. You can have herbal and flower plants in the north-east sector of the plot. Plants like *tulsi, thumbe, darbhe* grass (for lawns), and other herbal plants are good. Keep the north-east corner free.

Avoid having thorny plants like cactus etc. inside the house. I would personally recommend that they be totally done with. If you have a north or east facing house, you can have a beautiful pathway from your gate to the main door, with *tulsi* grown on the sides. *Darbhe* grass which is known to have potent healing powers can be grown in the pathway.

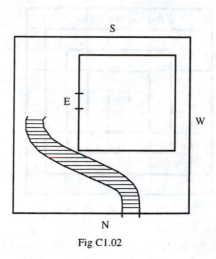

Fig C1.02

Avoid planting of trees in front of the main door.

Mezzanine floors if required should be in the south or west.

For rooms within the house try to have doors as far as possible in the east or north of north-east. Else you can have them in south of south-east and west of north-west.

Avoid doors in the south or west of south-west, north of north-west and east of south-east.

As for windows many scholars recommend even number of windows, preferably not being ten, twenty, etc. See that the surface area of north+east openings are greater than surface area of south+west openings.

As for the arrangement of the furniture inside the house, have the seating arrangements on the south and west as much as possible. Guests can be seated in the north-west sector of the rooms. The master of the house can always occupy the south or west if the furniture is placed on the south/west side facing either north or east.

Almirahs, wardrobes, treasure chests can be in the South - West of the rooms. This is the opinion of the modern scolars. (The classical texts opine that the "treasury" room be in the North.)

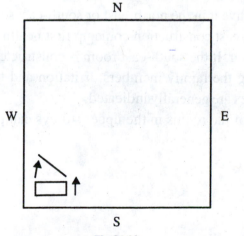

Fig C1.03

However if almirah and wardrobes are not possible in the South or West for any reason, only light articles have to be kept in them. Never put any loads in the north-east corners of the rooms. As already suggested cupboards containing property papers, profession documents, valueables, cash etc should be in the south-west corner of the master's room so that the cupboards open to the north. The northern room can be used to store cash, jewellery, etc.

Have your cots and beds in the south-west of the rooms, of course not touching the wall. Adults can have their heads to the south and the children to the west.

Lofts and attics is various room can be on the south and west of the rooms.

Balconies can preferably be for the north and east rooms. Avoid south and west, especially the south-west balconies. If you are residing in a house which already has a south-west balcony, get it covered with grills and cover it with curtains.

Terraces are always preferred on the north and east. If you plan to have a part construction on the first floor or second floor, have it on the south-west sector.

Never have it in the north-east or south-east sector. By having a north-east construction come up first health and finances tend to suffer. If the south-east room is constructed first bitterness among the family members, irritation and tensions over trivial issues are generally indicated.

Height of the rooms in the upper storeys can progressively decrease.

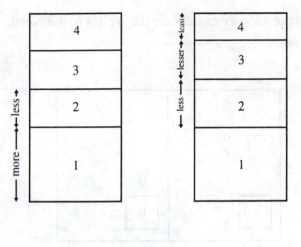

Fig C1.04

It is not adviseable to share a well between two houses.

Depending in the placement of the well, it may or may not be alright.

For example in the following figure, A is likely to have a well properly placed whereas B has it in an undesirable position.

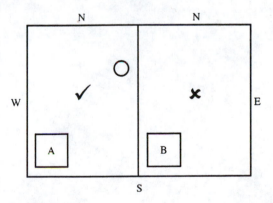

Fig C1.05

Let's take another case. Here the well is to the North-east of both the plots.

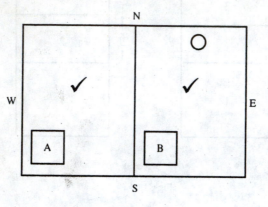

Fig C1.06

2. Apartments & Multistoreyed Buildings

> ### At a glance:
>
> *The dwelling is a living organism. A multistoreyed build-ing has rhythm and grace and can be compared to a musi-cal instrument. Select an apartment carefully and strengthen the interiors by suitable placements of furniture.*

Our ancients considered the dwelling to be a living organisa-tion with rythm in it. Proportion was of prime importance. Tem-ples with several storeys were built in such a way that the height of each storey decreased as it went up. The building is com-pared to a musical instrument whose distance between the strings reduce as they go up. Such a building is said to vibrate with rythm and grace.

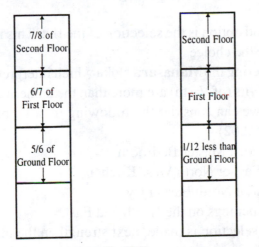

Fig C2.01

A multistoreyed building can be compared to a veena (a stringed musical instrument) in which the distance between the consecutive rods of the shaft reduces gradually to give the most melodius music. The following heights for the various floors can be followed.

First Floor	5/6 of Ground Floor
Second Floor	6/7 of First Floor
Third Floor	7/8 of Second Floor and so on.

This gradual and rythmic reduction in each floor will create a harmonious and uniform energy level in the entire building.

Brihat Samhita and **Matsyapurana** recommend a gradual reduction by 1/12th in each floor.

As the need for dwelling in the cities grows, more and more high rise buildings are coming up. The land developers are busy investing on others land (in the city) and jointly developing the properties. The main criteria is to make maximum use of land and vertical space and build as many apartments as possible. Many people wonder how vastu can be applied to already built apartments.

The first option is we have to go for a flat. Let us say this is fate.

The second option is the selection of the flat. This is freewill and we have the choice.

Remembering the **Manasara** sloka which interprets (partly) that if the merits (of Vastu) are more than the demerits, it is said to be good, we can consider the following in order of priority. (See figure C2.02)

1. South West Master Bedroom
2. South East or North West Kitchen
3. An East of North East entry
4. More openings on the North and East.

Once the selection is made, next strengthen the interiors as follows:

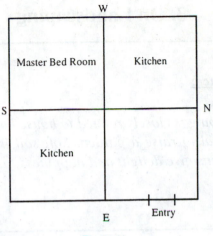

Fig C2.02

1. Sleep to the South West corner (without touching the walls) with the head to the South.

2. Arrange the furniture such that the north and east as well as the Brahmasthana of the rooms are free.

3. If wall sceneries are used have such ones that depict depth, distant seas, deep gardens, bubbling infants etc. on the north and east walls. Avoid beautifying your living areas with scenes depicting violence, terror, cruelty, stark poverty, death etc. — to put it simply avoid paintings and sceneries which depict the negative aspects of life.

This way the vastu strength can be enhanced to improve the general quality of one's life.

3. On Landscaping

At a glance:

Landscaping is closely related to house building. North west is sideal to raise a garden. Soft soil is suitable for trees. Gardens give delight and happiness to the residents and visitors.

Gardening or Landscaping has been connected closely with town planning and house building. Ancient sages have laid down certain rules for planting trees.

They always saw to it that houses were sorrounded by gardens containing a variety of trees and plants decorative and herbal.

It is said that the goddess of wealth lives for generations in the house in which the bilva (Aegle Marmelos) tree is planted.

It is also said that a man enjoys the fruits of virtue if he plants fruit and flower bearing trees.

A garden is normally recommended in the north-west sector of the house.

Trees can be planted in the months of Rohini, Uttaraphalguna, Uttarashada, Uttarabhadrapada, Chitra, Anuradha, Mrigasira, Revati, Moola, Visakha, Pushya, Sravana, Aswini and Hasta.

Saplings can be planted at a fair distance from each other — about 4 cubits (6ft.) apart. The distance between the saplings should neither be too close nor too far off. *ashoka* (Saraca Indica), *nimbaa* (lemon), *champaka* (Michelia) are some of the recommended trees.

Just as houses should have compounds, the ancients recommend that the trees be protected with walls.

Heavy leaf bearing trees can be planted in the south west with fruit trees in between them. Rock gardens if required can be in the south west region.

Herbal plants like tulsi, tumbe (a flower sacred to Lord Shiva) can be grown in the north-east region.

Brihat Samhita has much to say about gardens.

It states that soft soil is suitable for growth of trees. It mentions substance having properties of manure like dung of cows, buffaloes, sheep etc., sesamum, honey, milk, various types of cereals like green gram, black gram, barley, rice, etc.

Gardens (public gardens) are recommended on the banks of rivers and lakes. *Margosa* (neem), *ashoka* (Saraca Indica) *punnaga* (Calophyllum isophyllum), *sirisa* (Albizzia lebbeck) are recommended in one's garden and rear houses.

Grafting is done by smearing a branch with cowdung and transplanting it on the branch of another tree. The junction of the transplant is covered with a coating of mud.

Grafting is recommended for plants yet to grow branches in *Sirisa* (February-March), for plants that have grown branches in Hemanta (December-January) and for these that have large branches in Varsha (August-September).

"Export" grafting is also mentioned. Plants can be sent to other countries and grafted there. The plant to be exported should be smeared with a mixture of ghee, sesamum, andropogon honey, *Vidanga* (Embelia Ribes), milk and cow dung.

Tree diseases are treated as follows. The "ulcer" parts should be cleared with a knife. Then these parts should be applied with a paste of *Vidanga*, ghee and mud and then sprinkled with milk and water.

When fruit bearing trees do not yield fruits and when fruits are destroyed prematurely, the trees should be watered with cooled milk which has been boiled with horse gram, black gram, green gram, barley and sesamum.

This way the trees are said to regain their flower and fruit bearing strength.

The ancients gave much importance to laying of gardens and maintaining them. Gardens not only enhance the vastu srength of a building but also make it a delightful experience for the residents and the visitors to the house.

In fact *Vrkshayurveda* recommends artificially made caves adorned with branches of trees, leaves and creepers, artificial peaks etc!

SECTION IV

Your Questions Answered

<u>*At a glance:*</u>

Can trees be felled?
Is there a relationship between the length and breadth of a building?
Should we apply Ayadi Shadvarga to our homes already constructed?
   — Find out the answers for yourself.

Can trees be felled?

This is a question that is causing much unhappiness to many people who have already planted their trees in the north and east of the north-east sector. Personally speaking I do not feel that one or two trees planted in this region could disturb the Vastu balance.

Effective steps to strengthen the south-west sector by planting one or two additional trees can be taken. Of course if the Vedha or obstruction is caused to the mahadwara, we may perhaps have to think of a solution.

The ancients have prescribed a way of doing this.

Pooja to the tree has to be performed the previous night and offerings made. Next morning, after pooja again, the tree is ready to be felled. The tree may be so cut that it falls to its east or north.

Are irregular plots or structures recommended?

No. The classical works are very clear in stating that the structure should be a perfect square or a rectangle.

NORTH WEST	NORTH	NORTH EAST
WEST	BRAHMA	EAST
SOUTH WEST	SOUTH	SOUTH EAST

Fig D 1.01

In fact **Brihat Samhita** (Chp. LIII, Sloka 67 & 68) gives the following results.

दक्षिणाभुजेन हीने वास्तुनरेऽर्थयोऽङ्गनादोषाः ।
वामेऽर्थधान्यहानिः शिरसि गुणैर्हीयते सर्वैः ॥
स्त्रीदोषाः सुतमरणं प्रेष्यत्वं चापि चरणावैकल्ये ।
अविकलपुरुषे वसतां मानार्थयुतानि सौख्यानि ॥

1. When south east is cut, the owner will lose wealth and will be miserable through women.

2. When the north west is cut there is loss of money and food.

3. When north-east is cut he will fall from virtues.

4. When the south-west is cut there is death of male children, troubles through women and the master becomes servile.

5. On the other hand if all the angles are right the inmates of the house will be happy and live with wealth and honour.

Is there a relationship between the length and breadth of a building?

Yes, the best is a square structure where you have both the length and breadth equal. However this may not be possible in many cases. The rectangular structure is the choice.

Brihat Samhita states that the length of a king's dwelling should be greater than its breadth by a quarter.

For example the following table gives the lengths and breadth which can be used by you for your house.

Breadth	Length
In Feet	
18	22.5
20	25
25	31.25
30	37.50
40	50
45	56.25
50	62.50
80	100
100	125

Table D 1.01

It is to be noted that the maximum length of the building should be twice the breadth and no more.

What is the height recommended for buildings?

The **Brihat Samhita** recommends the height to be equal to its breadth.

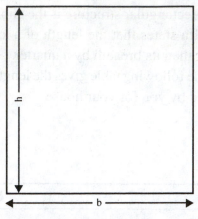

Fig D 1.02

Should we apply Ayadi Shadvarga to our homes already constructed?

I do not think it is necessary to scratch your head over a finished construction as far as the *ayadi* is concerned. In fact I would recommend the application of *ayadi shadvarga* for mansions, huge bungalows and public places.

Manasara is clear when it says that if the merits are more than the demerits (of vastu) it can be considered as not having any defect.

Do you recommend any specific measurement while using mirrors?

Always go in for square or rectangular (l=2b) mirrors. They can be hung on east and north walls of the house.

Can a plot be extended by purchasing the adjacent land?

Yes, of course as long as the adjacent land is towards the east, north or north-east of the original property and is an extension to the property. Avoid buying land to the south, west, southwest, north-west or south-east of your property.

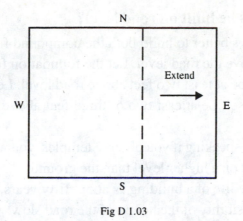

Fig D 1.03

Can a portion of the house be rented out?

Retain the south-west portion of the house and rent out the rest. Avoid letting out part of the house at the cost of retaining the north-west portion which could bitter your relationship with the tenant to your detriment. If it is an independent house rent out the total portion.

Which is the suitable site in a hill station for building a house?

Select a site where you have all elevations, rocks, mounds, heavy trees to the south and the west. Let the slope be towards the north and east. If there is a stream or river running on the north, east or north-east of your site, it is a good bargain.

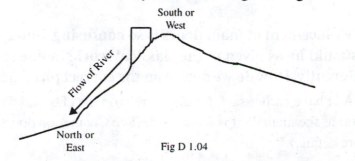

Fig D 1.04

Can houses be built on road level?

It is always better to build both the compound floor and the structure above the road level. Let the foundation for the compound floor be at least two feet above road level. Let the house (structure) itself be atleast two or three feet above the ground level.

Generally speaking if you observe temples, you will find that they are built on a higher level than the ground.

Taking the life of a building as about fifty years, there is always the possibility of the height of the road slowly increasing over a period of time. It is therefore all the more necessary that the structure is built at a higher height to avoid flow of rain water, etc., from the road into the building or compound.

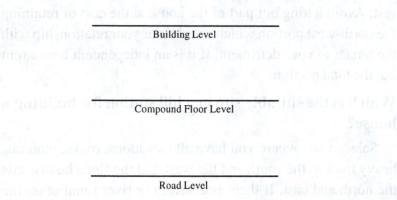

Building Level

Compound Floor Level

Road Level

Fig D 1.05

The placement of main doors is so confusing. Some say it should be as given in the classical works, some say it differently. How do we decide on the correct placement?

As I have earlier said, I prefer to rely on the classical works as far as the main door is concerned. (See Chapter on doors for more details)

However, in cases where it may not be possible to stick to this because of building constraints modern scholars suggest the following guidelines.

Favourable in	N-NE	E-NE	S-SE	W-NW
Unfavourable in	E-SE	W-SW	S-SW	N-NW

Table D 1.02

Is a peephole through the main door advisable ?

As a rule have a small window between the main door and the wall. This will enable the lady of the house to have a clear view of strangers pressing the door bell.

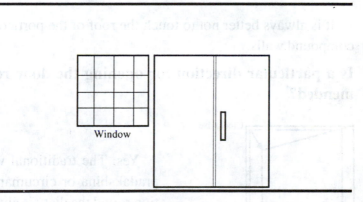

Window

Fig D 1.06

Is it advisable to have a pillar on the north-east corner to support a portico?

A cantilever roof which is slightly lower than the main roof is recommended. As the north-east corner corresponds to the Vastu Purusha's head and to the konasutras (energy lines running diagonally across the Brahmasthana from South west to North east and North west to south east — please refer to Fig 11.01 on page 48), a pillar or a load in this corner is better avoided.

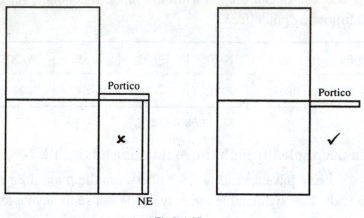

Fig D 1.07

It is always better not to touch the roof of the portico to the compound walls.

Is a particular direction for opening the door recommended?

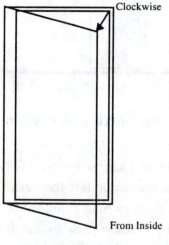

Fig D 1.08

Yes. The traditional way of pradakshina or circumambulation round the diety is always in the clockwise direction. Similarly when you stand inside the house, the main door should open towards your left, in the clockwise direction. As far as possible apply this principle for the other doors inside the house too.

As master of the house, which place do you recommend for me to sit?

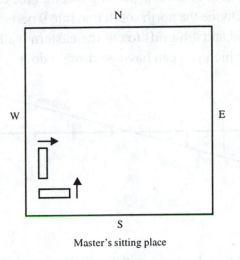

Master's sitting place

Fig D 1.09

Always occupy the south or west of the south-west of any room—living, kitchen or drawing for your seating. You can face east or north. Other members of the family also can seat them-selves such that they also face east or north only.

What pictures are suitable in my drawing room?

You can have natural sceneries which are pleasing to the eye on your north and east walls. Pictures of smiling children etc. can also decorate your house.

Avoid pictures depicting violence, wild beasts, sickly peo-ple, burning forests, fires etc.

Photos of departed souls can be hung on the south walls.

How do you define a door when the site and building is tilted 20° to the cardinal directions?

Let us suppose you have a slightly east facing site on which you construct a house.

Find out the centre point of the eastern wall on the plan. Tilt
the plan to the direction the site is facing. Put your compass on
it and draw a north-south line passing through the centre of the
eastern wall. Divide the north south line into 9 parts. Draw lines
on the 2nd, 3rd and 4th grids to cut the eastern wall. These are
the places at which you can have your main door.

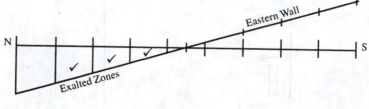

Fig D 1.10

What should the thickness of the walls of a building be ?

Brihat Samhita categorically mentions that the wall thickness should be 1/16th of the breadth of a building if it is made
out of bricks. For wooden houses no restriction is mentioned.

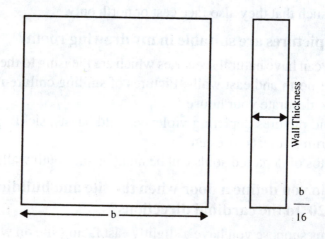

Fig D 1.11

Let us suppose that the breadth of a building in 32 feet. The thickness of the wall (inclusive of plastering) recommended is

$$32 \times \frac{1}{16} = 2'$$

Perhaps they considered this formula necessary to safeguard the building from thieves, dacoits etc.

Are pathways round the house good?

Brihat Samhita the great work of Varahamihira recommends a pathway around the house and prescribes its breadth as equal to one-third of the breadth of the living room (hall).

It speaks of *Sosnisa*—pathway in front of the house; *Saayaasraya* — pathway behind the house; *Saavastamba* — pathway on two sides; and *Susthita* — pathway laid on all four sides, and concludes that all the pathways are approved by the architects.

Many houses in the villages have verandahs round the house. Are they recommended?

Yes, the classical works recommend an unbroken verandah all round the house provided they have 4 doors on all the sides.

The *Sarvatobhadra* as the house is called is said be beneficial in all respects.

1) A house is called *Nandyaavarta* when it has verandahs on all sides going from left to right, each a separate one. It has three doors except on the west.

2) A house is called *Vardhamana* when the front verandah extends from left to right. Another verandah from there is from left to right and there is a third one again from left to right. There is no entrance on the south for a *Vardhamana* building.

3) A house is called *Swastika* when the western verandah extends from the left to the right. The other two verandahs

(southern and northern), originating from the western verandah should touch the ends in the east. The eastern verandah is held between them. The entrance should be in the east.

4) A house is called *Ruchaka* when the eastern and western verandahs touch the ends in the south and the north. There are two more verandahs touching these internally. Entrances in all the directions except north are recommended.

The *Nandyavarta* and *Vardhamana* are said to be the best apart from *Sarvatobhadra*.

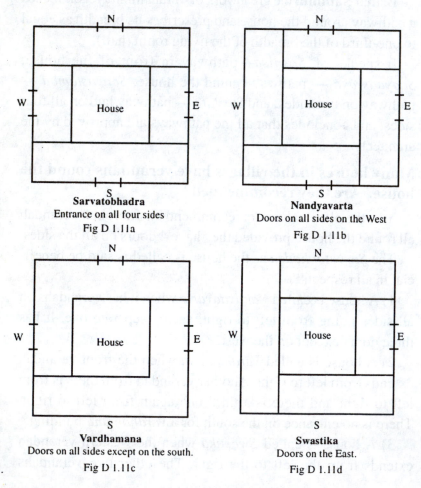

Sarvatobhadra
Entrance on all four sides
Fig D 1.11a

Nandyavarta
Doors on all sides on the West
Fig D 1.11b

Vardhamana
Doors on all sides except on the south.
Fig D 1.11c

Swastika
Doors on the East.
Fig D 1.11d

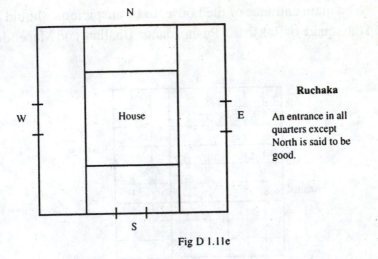

Fig D 1.11e

Can you suggest a general arrangement of the rooms?

The central South is for dining; the central North is for storing money; the South-east corner for the Kitchen and the North West for granary; the North-east corner for the prayer room as also the well; the East for baths; South West for the Master and West for Children.

	N	
GRANARY	STORE FOR MONEY	PRAYER ROOM AND WELL
CHILDREN	HALL	BATH
MASTER	DINING	KITCHEN

Fig D 1.12

The main entrance of the house, to be auspicious, should be on the square of Rakshasa, Pushpadanta, Bhallata and Mahendra.

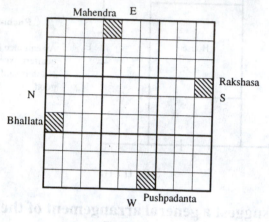

Fig D 1.13

Can the cots and other furniture have any sizes?

The classical works prescribe certain proportionate measurements. The ancients felt that *Vastu* was an important as the *Vaastu*.

The ratio recommended for a cot is 3:5. Suppose the Width of the cot is 4 ft., the ideal length will be 6.6 ft.

The length of the legs is prescribed as more than one hasta and less than one and a half hasta. This works out to 18" and 27" respectively. The legs have to be straight and can have feet in the shape of a tiger foot or a deer foot.

CONCLUSION

Vastu Shastra is intended to ensure the building up of a contented, prosperous and a happy society.

The ancients designed a set of *dos* and *don'ts* while constructing buildings or townships taking into consideration the interplay of various forms of energies radiated by man.

In a plot of land these energies, either positive or negative, are at perpetual play. The fields of energy get distorted when a building is constructed on the plot. The ancient sages in India after a great deal of contemplation and experimentation arrived at a certain way of construction such that the building worked in harmony with the energy fields rather than against them, in the process, making man a compatible part of the area/environment.

The human body has layers of aura or subtle energy levels. The strength or weakness of these energy levels depend on the evolution of the concerned individual. When the energy fields of the human body interact with the energy fields of the building, good and bad results follow.

Hence the ancients felt that it was all the more necessary to build a house such that the two energy levels, one of the animate and the other of the inanimate worked in harmony or resonance.

The science of Vastu also takes into consideration the *pancha mahabhootas*, viz., Prithvi (Earth), Apa (water), Agni (Fire), Vayu (Air) and Akasha (sky or space).

In Ayurveda when these *panchamahabhootas* are well balanced the body and mind are said to be in good health. Similarly when selecting a site and constructing a house, if these *pancha mahabhootas* are balanced the building and the people residing in it will be in good health and contented.

This way the ancients developed a methodology of contruction which ensured the happiness and peace of mind of the residents of the building.

The whole world will be a happier place to live in if Vastu is applied not only to construction of residences but also educational institutions, public buildings, religious places, layouts, complexes and satellite towns.

Town planning and development authorities would do well to consider the Vastu aspect before trying to expand the townships disproportionately.

SECTION V

SOME PLANS

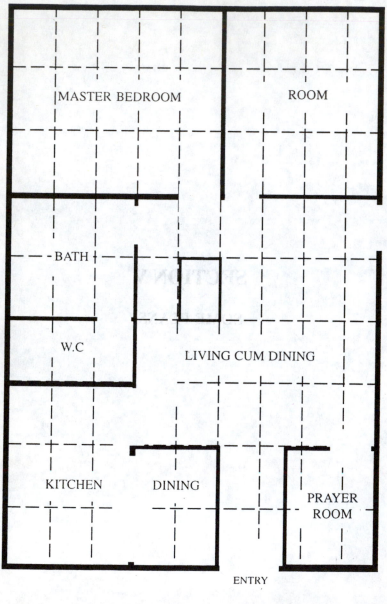

MASTER BEDROOM

ROOM

EXIT

BATH

W.C

LIVING CUM DINING

KITCHEN   DINING

PRAYER ROOM

ENTRY

20 feet x 30 feet east facing plot

This is a house in a 20' x 30' plot. The plot faces the East Road. The whole area is treated for construction as the space is too small.

However if you can, you may allow 3' of space on the east and the northern sides and 2' of space on the western and southern sides.Consequently the dimensions of inner rooms will reduce.

The building area is divided into 81 cells or grids. The central nine grids are called the Brahmasthana.

The main entry in the east is given on the third and fourth grids from the north side.

An exit door which is essential for cross ventilation may be provided in the fourth grid on the north side from the west side.

The house is so designed that the Brahmasthana is used as a general lounge area. No beams or pillars should come in the central nine grids.

The plan may be used with suitable modifications depending on whether the road is south, east or west.

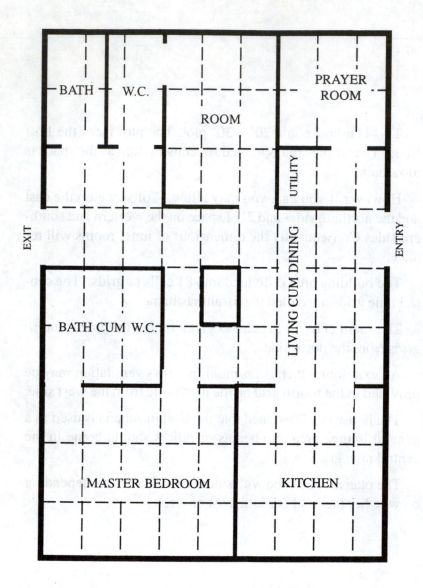

40 feet x 60 feet south facing plot

This is a house in a 40' x 60' plot. The plot faces the south road.

All round the building a minimum of 6 and a half feet on the north and south sides and 5 feet 5inches on the east and west are left free. This free space comes under the *Paisacha* zone.

The building area is divided into 81 cells or grids. The central nine grids are called the Brahmasthana.

The plan is designed to give two bedrooms and two toilets.

The main entry in the east falls in the fourth grid from the north side. A corresponding exit door which is essential for cross ventilation is provided on the western wall exactly opposite the entry.

The house is so designed that the Brahmasthana is used as a general lounge area. No beams or pillars should come in the central nine grids.

A utility area is provided next to the prayer room.

The plan may be used with suitable modifications depending on whether the road is north, east or west.

> *The plans on the following pages relate only to smaller plots. Once the cocept is understood, the reader may extend the principles to larger plots.*

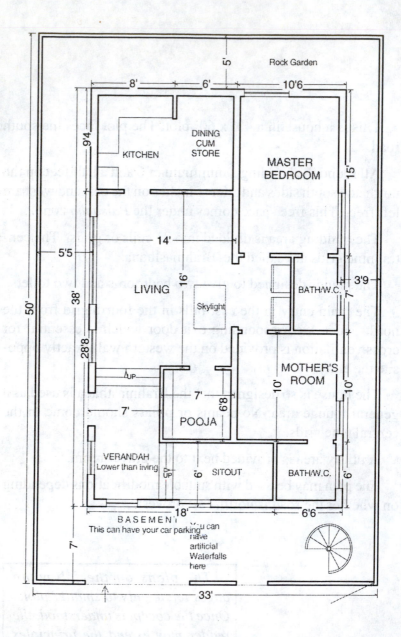

50'

Rock Garden

8'   6'   10'6

9'4

KITCHEN

DINING CUM STORE

MASTER BEDROOM

15'

5'5

14'

16'

LIVING

Skylight

BATH/W.C.

3'9

7'

38'

28'8

MOTHER'S ROOM

UP

10'

10'

7'   7'

6'8

POOJA

VERANDAH
Lower than living

UP   SITOUT

9'   6'

BATH/W.C.

6'

18'   6'6

BASEMENT
This can have your car parking   You can have artificial Waterfalls here

7'

33'

This house is designed in a plot of 33' x 50' with a north road. A minimum of 1/9th space (3'9"x5'6") is left open all around. The centre of the building has a skylight to allow sunlight into the living area. The entrance to the house is on the eastern wall in the north east portion. A circular staircase is provided in the north west. The car parking is in the cellar in the north-east sector (below the verandah and living). The house has two bedrooms with attached toilets.and a small sitout facing the road.

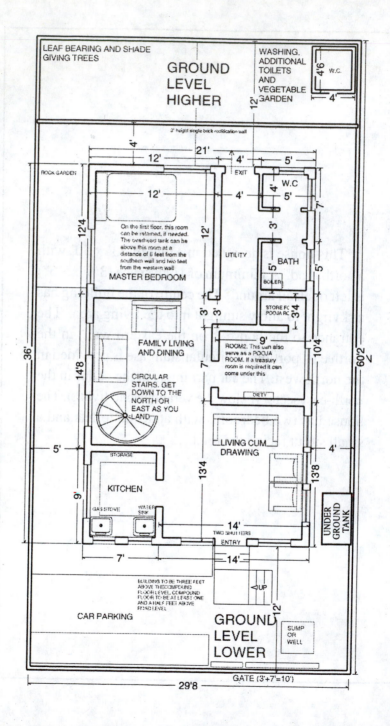

This house is designed in a plot of 30' x 60' with an east road. A minimum of 1/9th space is left open all around. The entrance to the house is on the eastern wall in the north east portion. As the owner needed only one room more area for lawn space was provided. An internal staircase is provided in the south east. The car parking is in the south-east sector. A sump in the north of north-east is provided.

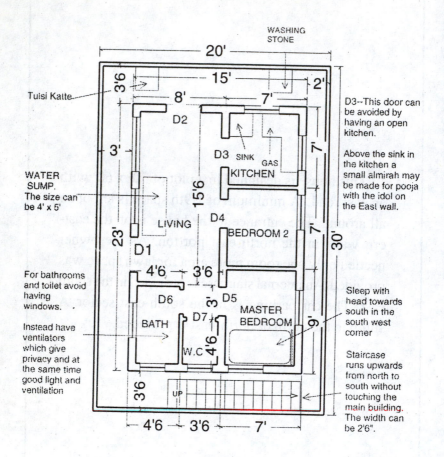

Tulsi Katte

WATER SUMP. The size can be 4' x 5'

For bathrooms and toilet avoid having windows.

Instead have ventilators which give privacy and at the same time good light and ventilation

WASHING STONE

20'
15'
3'6
2'
8'
7'
D2
3'
D3   SINK
GAS
KITCHEN
15'6
23'
LIVING
D4
BEDROOM 2
7'
7'
30'
D1
4'6
3'6
D6
3'
D5
9'
BATH
D7
MASTER BEDROOM
W.C
4'6
3'6
UP
4'6
3'6
7'

D3--This door can be avoided by having an open kitchen.

Above the sink in the kitchen a small almirah may be made for pooja with the idol on the East wall.

Sleep with head towards south in the south west corner

Staircase runs upwards from north to south without touching the main building. The width can be 2'6".

This house is designed in a plot of 20' x 30' with a west road. A minimum of 1/9th space is left open all around. The entrance to the house is on the northern wall in the prescribed zone viz., Kusumadanta. Apart from the main room a small room in the northern region can work either as a treasury room or a study room. The living comes in the north east of the room. As the plot itself is of small dimensions, a sump (underground) tank is provided in the north of north-east inside the house.

This a two bedroom house.

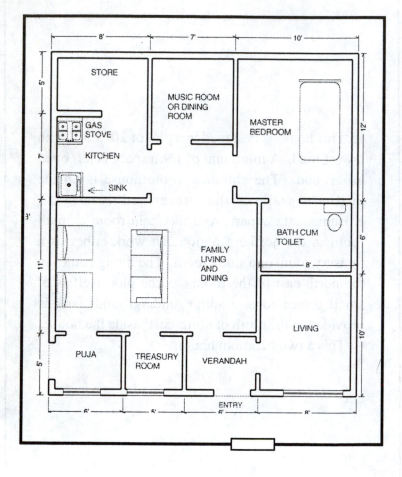

This house is designed in a plot of 28' x 36' with a north road. A minimum of 1/9th space is left open all around. The entrance to the house is on the northern wall in the prescribed zone viz., Kusumadanta. Apart from the main room a small room in the northern region can work either as a treasury room or a study room. Entry is into a small verandah and to the right you have the living. On the south you have a music room which can also be your dining.

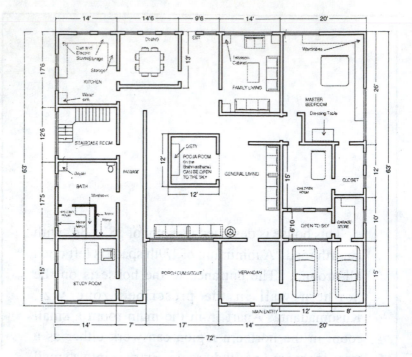

This house is designed in a plot of 100' x 100' with a north road. A minimum of 1/9th space is left open all around. The entrance to the house is on the northern wall in the prescribed zone viz., Kusumadanta. The outer dimensions of the house are 63'x72'. The prayer room is situated in the centre (in the Brahmasthana). The master room is in south-west (20'x26'). Close to the master room is the child room (15'x12') and the closet (8'x12') is common to both the rooms. The north-east has the study-room (15'x14'). The kitchen (14'x17'6") has a dining hall (14'6"x13'). The exit to the backyard is through the Brahatakshata. The staiircase room (12'6"x14') is next to the kitchen. The north-west has the garage (15'x20') which has a door into the verandah (15'x14'). The garage has a store(8'x10') which has a door into the open space where a flower garden can be grown.. The front of the house has a porch-cum-sitout (17'x15'). Behind the prayer room is a six-feet high holed decorative wall which conceals the staircase and other rooms.

Index

REFERENCES

References include various originals and translations of works like Manasara, Mayamata, Samarangana Sutradhara, Viswakarma Prakasha, Brihat Samhita, Matsya and other puranas, Kautilya's Arthasastra, Silpa Sastra, Mahabharatha and Ramayana Epics, Prasna Marga translated by Dr. B. V. Raman, How to Judge a Horoscope Vol. I & II, Muhurtha and other books of Dr. B. V. Raman, THE ASTROLOGICAL MAGA-ZINE and many other scholarly works by eminent ancient and modern writers.

OTHER BOOKS ON
ASTROLOGY AND PALMISTRY
in UBSPD

		Rs
Raman, B V	A Catechism of Astrology 4/e	45.00
Raman, B V	A Manual of Hindu Astrology 16/e	50.00
Raman, B V	Astrology in Predicting Weather and Earthquakes	35.00
Raman, B V	Ashtakavarga System of Prediction	45.00
Raman, B V	Astrology for Beginners 26/e	25.00
Raman, B V	Bhavartha Ratnakara 10/e	45.00
Raman, B V	Graha and Bhava Balas 13/e	40.00
Raman, B V	Hindu Astrology and the West 5/e	50.00
Raman, B V	Hindu Predictive Astrology 20/e	50.00
Raman, B V	My Experiences in Astrology	60.00
Raman, B V	Planets and the Next World War	60.00
Raman, B V	Planetary Influences on Human Affairs 12/e	45.00
Raman, B V	Prasna Tantra	50.00
Raman, B V	Raman's 110 Year Ephemeris of Planetary Positions (1891 to 2000 A.D.) 10/e	50.00
Raman, B V	Varshaphal or the Hindu Progressed Horoscope 13/e	45.00
Raman, B V	Muhurtha - Electional Astrology	50.00

*Prices are subject to change.